LON█████'S
LOST MUSIC VENUES 2

PAUL TALLING

DG
BOOKS

ONLY ONES 8/3/81
FAREWELL GIG LYCEUM
NO. D·C90

DELTA 5 LYCEUM

JOY DIVISION LYCEUM 29/2/80

THE WILLING SINNERS 2
hammersmith Palais thurday 31 Jan 85

Public Image Ltd HAMMERSMITH PALAIS
22/11/83

RAMONES LYCEUM
Tuesday 26th. Feb. 85

(P L) HAMMERSMITH PALAIS 22.11.83

Jonathan Richman VENUE, VICTORIA.
20TH MAY 1982

THE STRAY CATS LYCEUM

  SUBWAY SECT LYCEUM chrom-dioxid 120
SPIZZLES 22·2·81 (M)

LONDON's
LOST MUSIC VENUES 2

First published in Great Britain in 2022 by Damaged Goods Books
Damaged Goods Books 45 Colworth Road London E11 1JA

ISBN: 978-1-9162327-1-6

Disclaimer.
The author and publisher take no responsibility for any errors, omissions, or contradictions which may exist in the book.

Printed and bound in China by C&C Offset Printing Co. Ltd.

Distributed to the trade by Turnaround Publisher Services www.turnaround-uk.com

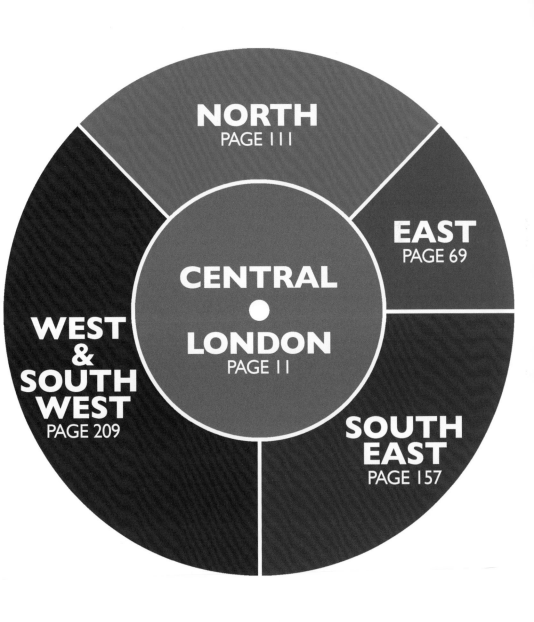

STRAIGHT MUSIC PRESENTS

THE POLICE
THE CRAMPS
BOBBY HENRY
LYCEUM
STRAND, W.C.2
EXTRA CONCERT
SUNDAY 17th JUNE at 7.30
LONDON THEATRE BOOKINGS, SHAFTESBURY AVE., TEL. 439 3371, PREMIER BOX OFFICE, TEL. 240 2245,
OR ROCK ON RECORDS, 3 KENTISH TOWN RD. NW1, TEL. 485 5056

TONY BULLIMORE PRESENTS
1st UK tour of the legendary superstar
BIG YOUTH
Backed by his own group
from Kingston J.A.
THE ARK ANGELS
Plus the sensational
DENNIS BROWN
WITH
JOE GIBBS AND THE
PROFESSIONALS
RAINBOW THEATRE
LONDON   Thurs 8th Sept
£5, £4, £3   Fri 9th Sept
                  Sat 10th Sept

NEW YORK DOLLS
CHRISTMAS BALL

MON. 26th NOV. & TUES. 27th NOV. 8   12–30
THE RAINBOW RESTAURANT, BIBAS
KENSINGTON HIGH ST. LONDON S.W.8.
BEGGARS OPERA · LUCAS & McCULLOUGH   your DJ Jerry Floyd

STRAIGHT MUSIC PRESENTS
ROCKPILE
FEATURING
DAVE EDMUNDS & NICK LOWE
WITH GUESTS
LEW LEWIS REFORMER · THE SPECIALS
HAMMERSMITH PALAIS
TUESDAY 26th JUNE at 8·00
TICKETS £3.50 IN ADVANCE PALAIS BOX OFFICE, TEL: 748 2812
LONDON THEATRE BOOKINGS, SHAFTESBURY AVE., TEL. 439 3371, PREMIER BOX OFFICE, TEL: 240 2245,
OR ROCK ON RECORDS, 3 KENTISH TOWN RD. NW1, TEL. 485 5056

HARVEY GOLDSMITH ENTERTAINMENTS
THE
ONLY ONES
SPECIAL GUESTS
BRAM TCHAIKOVSKY'S
BATTLEAXE
THE BUSINESS
LYCEUM BALLROOM
THE STRAND
SUNDAY 1st OCTOBER at 7.15pm
Tickets £2.00 in advance
£2.25 on door

oasis
PLUS SPECIAL GUESTS
LONDON EARLS COURT
THURSDAY 25th SEPTEMBER 1997 DOORS OPEN 5.30PM SHOW STARTS 7.00
PRICE £18.50 (+£1 subject to booking fee)
STANDING

HARVEY GOLDSMITH
ENTERTAINMENTS
PRESENTS
at the LYCEUM
PENETRATION
with special guests
The Fall
Ed Banger and His Group Therapy
+ Punishment of Luxury
Sunday 30th August £2 in advance £2.25 on door
Doors open 7.15 p.m.
Tickets available from the Box Office, Lyceum Ballroom.

MISTY   SHAM 69
DESPERATE BICYCLES
HILL NEW CAVENDISH ST. W1

RAINBOW THEATRE
FINSBURY PARK
KENNEDY STREET ARTISTES presents
ELVIS COSTELLO & The Attractions
at 6.30 p.m.
Thursday DEC 24
CIRCLE
Incl. VAT   (Elvis will be on stage at 7.30pm) £4.50
Gravesend, Kent.

FRIDAY 28th MARCH
NO
NUKES
MUSIC
JOHN COOPER CLARKE
ESSENTIAL LOGIC
THE IVORY BIRDS

CROCKETT'S
wednesday
18th february
london borderline
(orange yard, manette st, w1)
doors 8.30pm / show till 11 / bar till 2pm

PETER
TOSH
RAINBOW THEATRE

Manicured Noise
The Teardrop Explodes
Psychedelic Furs
A Certain Ratio
Echo & The Bunny Men
LYCEUM
SUNDAY 23rd MARCH at 6.30pm
TICKETS £2.50 IN ADVANCE

DAYS
ELEPHANT WITCH
butterfly
child
SOUND RELIEF PRESENTS
WED 11th OCT — LIVERPOOL SU   051 709 4047
WEDS 14th OCT — READING TU CLUB   0734 586506
FRI 16th OCT — LONDON ASTORIA

NEW FAST
AUTOMATIC
DAFFODILS

MINK DeVILLE
WITH GUESTS
TYLA GANG
RAINBOW THEATRE
SUN. 25th SEPTEMBER at 8·00

ORCHID BALLROOM
PURLEY
MECCA DANCING
Uplands 1174
Presenting on
Wednesday, 26th October
EDWIN STARR
Dancing 7.30-11 p.m — Admission 5/-

GREAT WESTERN
FESTIVALS
PRESENTS
in concert
MAN
WITH
QUICKSAND
Plus, a special presentation
A NUNDERMIME
ALMOST JACK AND THE
BEANSTALK
LYCEUM, STRAND

Lemonheads
plus WALT MINK and TUMBLE WEED
Thursday 15th October 7.30pm
ASTORIA
157 Charing Cross Rd, London WC1

STRAIGHT MUSIC PRESENTS
ADAM &
THE ANTS
TOYAH
PROTEX
Sunday 5th August at 7.30

Rainbow
THEATRE
232 Seven Sisters Rd, London W.4.
SUNDAY 1st OCTOBER 7.30pm.
Jimmy Cliff
ADMISSION
£1.50, £1.25, £1.00, 75p.
Tickets available in advance from Rainbow Theatre
Box Office 01-272 2224 and usual ticket agents

Mike & The Mechanics
Hanover House
6 Hanover Street
London W1R 9HH
Monday 10th May 19
Doors 7.30
Show 8.15
COMPETITION WIN

JVC presents
STIFF
LITTLE
FINGERS
PLUS Starjets AND THE VAPOURS
HAMMERSMITH PALAIS · SUNDAY 5th August 7.30pm.
TICKETS £2.50 ADVANCE £3.00 DOOR

Harvey Goldsmith Entertainments in
association with Cowbell present
SHAM'S
LAST STAND

SHAM 69
with
special guests
The Low Numbers and Others
RAINBOW FINSBURY PARK
SATURDAY 28th July at 7.30pm

STRAIGHT MUSIC PRESENTS
PRETENDERS
MADNESS
INTERVIEW
Lyceum Strand
WC2
Sunday 29th July at 7.30

208 Rock
at the UK's finest ballroom
HAMMERSMITH PALAIS, W.6
"Sunday Nite Fever" Every Sunday
Sunday September 2nd
Doors open 8pm-2am
LIVE ON STAGE
HI TENSION
All the Fox Jocks, Alan Sullivan, Owen, Clinton &
Kelly's Road Show

ROYAL
HIGH ROAD
TOTTENHAM
Tel: 808 6291
RESIDENT
THE
MOVING
FINGER

MECCA DANCING
TONIGHT
7·30 - 11·30 p.m.
Adm. 7/6
SPRINGFIELD
PARK

FRIDAY 7th MARCH
7·30 - 11·30 p.m.
Adm. 7/6
AMEN
CORNER
FRIDAY 14th MARCH 7·30 - 11·30 p.m. Adm. 10/-
From U.S.A. THE TYMES

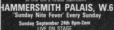

Introduction

As with the first volume, this book is not a social analysis of the scenes but more of a celebration of venues over the years whilst observing how many live music venues have disappeared and to answer the often asked question of what do those venues look like these days.

This second volume features the bigger halls and theatres as well as a few smaller venues not already included in the first volume plus some more recent losses.

I run walking tours all over London covering lost music venues, lost rivers & dereliction. To be notified of future dates, you can join the mailing list by emailing paul@derelictlondon.com. I also welcome your contributions of any old photographs and flyers/tickets/ads for venues which could be used in any future updates of this book.

Thank you for reading, and I hope to meet you at a gig or on one my walking tours soon! As ever, get out and support live music venues, both large and small.

We don't always fully appreciate these places until we lose them.

Paul Talling 2022

CENTRAL ● LONDON

Africa Centre

38 King Street, Covent Garden, WC2E 8JS

The Africa Centre was opened in 1964 in what was once a fruit and vegetable warehouse for the Covent Garden market. It became the focus for independence movements and the anti-apartheid campaign hosting a variety of cultural events in the 200-person capacity hall.

The Centre held nights hosting DJs and African live acts and from 1983. The Limpopo Club became a long-running regular night at the Centre hosting many live music performances from African acts including Ras Natty Baby, Kanda Bongo Man, Mzwakhe Mbuli and Youssou N'Dour. The Bhundu Boys played their UK debut here in 1987. From the mid-1980s Jazzie B would bring his Soul II Soul sound system to the Centre. The centre was hired out to outside promoters who sporadically put on non-African acts. In 1979 The The made their debut here third on the bill to Scritti Politti and PragVEC. The Psychedelic Furs played here the same year. In 1981 The Birthday Party played here twice and during the 1990s Suede and Flowered Up both played here. In 2012, there was a gig by alt-J.

Despite a campaign to save the Centre at its original premises, supported by Archbishop Desmond Tutu, the trustees of the Africa Centre decided that the building was no longer a viable home as it was too costly to maintain, and it moved to new premises in South London in 2013. The Life Force Band played the last ever gig at the Covent Garden venue.

The building is now occupied by the first UK branch of Mariage Frères who are France's oldest tea house, who claim that it offers the largest collection of teas in the world along with a tea museum.

Africa Centre

London Astoria

157 Charing Cross Road, Soho, WC2H 0EW

In 1927, the Astoria Picture Theatre and Dance Hall opened on the site using the brick shell of the warehouse of a former Cross and Blackwell pickle warehouse built in 1893.

After its failings as a theatre, it hosted a couple of gigs in 1984 by Carmel and INXS before all the seats in the stalls were removed. It reopened in 1985 as a nightclub and live music venue with a capacity for 2,000 people. Richey Edwards played his last gig with the Manic Street Preachers here in 1994 before going missing and U2 played a low-key gig here in 2001 with touts selling tickets outside for £2000. Other notable acts to have played include: Nirvana, Eminem, The Prodigy, Ash, Supergrass, Foals, The Kills, Muse and Rancid. In fact, who didn't play at the Astoria in its heyday?

Live performances recorded at the Astoria from the 1990s have been released on DVD including those by Billy Idol, David Bowie, Radiohead, Hard-Fi, Twisted Sister, Sum 41, Eels, Arctic Monkeys, The Smashing Pumpkins and a Steve

Marriott Memorial concert featuring Paul Weller and Noel Gallagher. Club nights included The Trip during the late 1980s at the height of acid house and G-A-Y from 1993, billed as London's largest gay club night when high profile acts including Madonna, McFly, Kylie Minogue, Westlife, Amy Winehouse and Boyzone all performed live PAs at the club. Another gay nightclub named OMO briefly took over and hosted live PAs by Kelly Rowland and Lady Gaga after G-A-Y relocated to Heaven nightclub in 2008.

A Compulsory Purchase Order was served on the building, and all the other properties on this corner block on Charing Cross Road and Oxford Street in order that they could all be demolished for construction work on a new Elizabeth Line Crossrail station for Tottenham Court Road. The Astoria closed for good in 2009 and was promptly demolished. The final night was a charity concert featuring The Automatic, My Vitriol, Frank Turner, ...And You Will Know Us by The Trail of Dead and The King Blues. Construction work on the site called Soho Place above the new station includes the creation of a new 600 seat theatre.

RAMONES
ASTORIA WEDNESDAY 28 JUNE
FROM 7.30PM £10.50 IN ADVANCE

RIVERMAN BY ARRANGEMENT WITH ITB
presents

GREEN DAY
PLUS SPECIAL GUESTS
AT
THE ASTORIA THEATRE
157 CHARING CROSS ROAD
LONDON WC2
SATURDAY 22nd OCTOBER 1994
TICKETS £7.00 Adv.   DOORS 7.00pm
01585

MCP Presents
SPARKS
LONDON ASTORIA
157 CHARING CROSS ROAD
LONDON WC2
SATURDAY 6th DECEMBER 1997
DOORS 7.00pm   TICKETS £11.00 ADVANCE
SPARKS ON STAGE 8pm SHARP
00721

Bandstand in assoc. with Performance present
SIGUE SIGUE SPUTNIK
LAST of the TEENAGE IDOLS
ASTORIA THEATRE
Charing Cross Road
THURS 17th
NOVEMBER

Astoria Theatre
157 Charing Cross Road, London WC2

RIVERMAN presents
Nirvana + Supports
Tuesday 5th November 1991
Doors Open 7.00 pm
UNRESERVED
£7.00 (incl VAT)
N° 0812

SONIC YOUTH
PLUS SUPPORT
at the ASTORIA THEATRE
157 Charing Cross Road, London WC2H 0EN
Sunday 16th October 1988
Tickets £6.50
DOORS OPEN 7pm
N° 1539

15

London Astoria 2/Sundown/Mean Fiddler

165 Charing Cross Road, Soho, WC2H 0EW

This was located in the basement of the London Astoria in what was originally The Astoria Ballroom. In 1972 the Rank Organisation converted this and three other sites into live venues and discos called Sundown Clubs. The others were the old Regal Cinema in Edmonton, The Odeon in Mile End and the Astoria in Brixton (now the O2 Academy).

The Charing Cross Road Sundown Club was primarily used as a disco but did host some performances by The Damned, 999, The Adverts, Steel Pulse, Generation X and the New Hearts in 1977 and The Comsat Angels, Duran Duran and Spandau Ballet in and around 1981-82.

From 1976 the club held a gay club called Bang! which changed its name to G-A-Y in the early 1990s increasing to two nights a week during the weekdays with another two nights at the weekend at the larger Astoria upstairs.

In 1982 the Sundown became Busby's Disco with a few live acts such as Flesh for Lulu and The Shamen playing there later that decade before becoming the LA2 (aka London Astoria 2), which by 1991/2 was putting on regular gigs by the likes of Zodiac Mindwarp and the Love Reaction, Pendragon, Marc Almond and Gallon Drunk. Numerous acts played here throughout the nineties including Suede, Shed Seven, Green Day, Drugstore, Asian Dub Foundation, The Bluetones, Reef, Skunk Anansie, EMF, Korn, 3 Colours Red, The Wannadies, Biohazard, The Lemonheads, No Doubt and Sick of It All. Metallica played a secret gig in 1995.

In 2000 the club was renamed the Mean Fiddler (previously the name of the owner's original Harlesden venue) with gigs continuing as before. Acts that played during this period included Magnum, Backyard Babies, GWAR, dEUS, The Wombats, Bloc Party, Dinosaur Jr, Jamiroquai, The Fratellis, Reuben, Bob Mould and The Kooks.

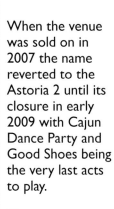

When the venue was sold on in 2007 the name reverted to the Astoria 2 until its closure in early 2009 with Cajun Dance Party and Good Shoes being the very last acts to play.

The reason for closing and subsequent demolition of the venue, as with the London Astoria upstairs, was for construction work on a new Elizabeth Line Crossrail station for Tottenham Court Road.

Bagley's/Canvas

Stable Street, Kings Cross, N I C 4DQ

Built in the 1850s as the Eastern Coal Drops this building was designed for coal wagons to enter on the top floor and drop their loads into loading carts below. By the end of the century this building had been turned into a warehouse by bottle and glass merchant Bagley's, and later it was used as a film studio.

From 1991 Bagley's became a multi-room club with a capacity of 2,500 people holding all-night rave parties mainly focused around DJs but they did host occasional live bands such as The Shamen and Sabres of Paradise. In 1993 Prince performed here at 5am for his Wembley Arena aftershow gig. The Rolling Stones used the club in 1995 to shoot their Like a Rolling Stone video. The Stranglers played a fan club convention gig in 1996 as did Suede in 1997. An all-nighter called Rockabilly Rave took place in 1996 with live guests The Go Getters and Jesse James and The Outlaws.

In 2003, Bagley's was taken over the and the name was changed to Canvas which continued as a popular dance club. Red Hot Chili Peppers, Bullet for My Valentine, Campag Velocet and Reuben played at events there and there was the TDK Cross Central Festival every year from 2004 to 2007 which also took over the adjacent clubs, The Cross and The Key and the Courtyard. Among many DJs there were live acts who included Goldfrapp, Friendly Fires, Battle, Archie Bronson Outfit, Robots in Disguise, Kosheen, The Kills, Courtney Pine, LCD Soundsystem, Ladytron, The Egg and Grace Jones. Canvas also hosted a weekly roller disco which can be seen in Madonna's Sorry video.

New Year's Day 2008 saw the closure of Canvas and the old warehouse and its vicinity is now reborn as an upmarket retail and leisure complex called the Coal Drops Yard.

To celebrate their 20 years playing rockabilly in the clubs ....

Tom Ingram & Jerrys Chatabox present

The Mid Summers All Night

ROCKABILLY RAVE!

Live on stage:

THE GO GETTERS

Jesse James & The Outlaws

VI

Plus Record Hops:
Jerrys Chatabox
Tom Ingram
Cosmic Keith

Saturday
10
August 96

At: Bagleys Ballroom
Goods Way (off York Way)
Kings Cross, London N1

10 pm
'til
6 am

Security By ShowTime

Details from: Tom (0181) 661 6555   Jerry (0181) 641 1785   GigLine (0891) 665090

Above - Bagley's 2013

WELCOME TO COAL DROPS YARD

Bagley's 2020

Borderline

Orange Yard, 16 Manette Street, Soho, W1D 4JB

This 300-capacity club just off the Charing Cross Road opened in 1985.

Acts who played here on the way to wider success include Lenny Kravitz, Texas, Crowded House, Rage Against the Machine, Pulp, PJ Harvey, Muse, Tori Amos, The Verve, Blur, Jane's Addiction and Pearl Jam. Many worldwide already established acts chose The Borderline to play intimate gigs including Spinal Tap, John Mellencamp, Oasis who also used the club for their "Cigarettes and Alcohol" video and Deborah Harry who played 8 nights here in 1989. R.E.M played two 'secret gigs' here in 1991 under the pseudonym Bingo Hand Job.

The Borderline was one of the last remaining live music venues in Soho and closed in August 2019 with American alternative rockers Night Riots playing on the final night. The owners cited increasing rents and ongoing redevelopment plans for Soho as the reason for closing, and they decided to reinvest the money into their other venues which include The Garage in Highbury, the Thekla in Bristol and Rock City in Nottingham.

The Borderline is now a nightclub called Orange Yard with high profile DJs but no live music. It has a 6am licence, which the owner claims is the latest in the area.

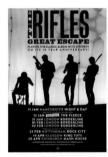

Bumpers

Corner House, 7-14 Coventry Street, Piccadilly Circus, W1D 7DH

Previously called the Trocadero Palace Music Hall when J Lyons & Co purchased the building in 1895 and converted it into the first of a chain of teashops & restaurants known as Lyons' Corner Houses. From the 1920s to the 1940s they presented cabaret and revues in the Grill Room which was what remained of the old Music Hall.

Mecca took over in 1965 and the grill room became a bowling alley and a nightclub called Bumpers.

From 1970 Bumpers put on a number of up-and-coming and already established acts including The Velvet Underground, Status Quo, The Coasters, Natural Acoustic Band, Jack Bruce, The Sweet, Geno Washington and The New Ram Jam Band and Slade.

A Melody Maker review in 1971 commented "There's something strange about that place" when reviewing a half full Mungo Jerry gig and noting that recent shows by The Kinks and Elton John had also recently failed to sell-out the club.

Around 1972 there was a fire which gutted the club and by 1984 a vast entertainment and shopping complex called the Trocadero was developed which incorporated the Corner House and its adjoining buildings.

Café de Paris

3-4 Coventry Street, W1D 6BL

The Café de Paris opened in 1924 and was initially frequented by the upper classes who included the then Prince of Wales, and the Aga Khan.

Over the years its audience became more mixed and by the Second World War the clientele often included members of the armed forces on leave. Despite being situated in a basement the café was bombed in 1941 during a performance and 31 people were killed when two bombs fell down a ventilation shaft and exploded in front of the stage. Two of the victims were bandleader Ken "Snakehips" Johnson and his saxophonist Dave "Baba" Williams.

After the war Café de Paris built a reputation as one of the leading clubs in London, hosting cabaret and live performers including Judy Garland, Josephine Baker, Marlene Dietrich, Frank Sinatra and Ava Gardner. In recent decades the venue has hosted a wide variety of popular live acts including Heaven 17, Jimmy Page and Robert Plant, Marc Almond, Prince, Cyndi Lauper, Daryl Hall and John Oates, Pink, Patti Smith, Rita Ora, Kylie Minogue and Bruno Mars. Between 2014 and 2019 the venue hosted an official run-up event to the Eurovision Song Contest where over 20 acts performed. In 2019 eventual Eurovision winner Duncan Laurence from the Netherlands played the event.

It's different—It's fabulous
The Newest West End Rendezvous
for
TRADITIONAL JAZZ
every Thursday, at the world-famous

Cafe de Paris
COVENTRY STREET · W.1

Next Thursday, 22nd May
AL FAIRWEATHER
AND HIS BAND AND THE
ART COPPERSMITH Jazzband
7.30—11.30 p.m. 5/-
You need pay nothing else
except cloakroom fee.
LICENSED
THE IDEAL ESTABLISHMENT FOR
LISTENERS AND DANCERS TO
TRADITIONAL JAZZ
Resident Manager: WALLY GREEN

The venue's opulent interior decor with a grand staircase and huge chandeliers made it a popular location for filming. Scenes from the films Absolute Beginners and The Krays were shot here as was the music video for I Think We're Alone Now by Girls Aloud.

Café de Paris closed down for good in 2020 after going into liquidation following the Covid-19 pandemic.

The Cat's Whisker

I Kingly Street, Soho, W1B 5PA

This was one of Soho's first coffee bars and was one of the earliest to have a jukebox. It catered for people on their way to or from the nearby theatres. In 1956 the bar's cellar was refurbished to cater for Spanish dancing with regular performances from guitarist Jose Feller but this soon gave way to skiffle and rock 'n roll. Many unknowns regularly played here before going on wider success such as Terry Dene, Cliff Richard, Lonnie Donegan, Tommy Steele and the Chas McDevitt Skiffle Group.

The Cat's Whisker at one time was so busy that, at the height of its popularity, according to Coca-Cola, it was the company's biggest single customer in the UK. Hand-jiving is said to have originated in this bar during performances by Leon Bell and the Bell Cats because of the lack of dancing space. The hand jive then caught on in the US helped by Johnny Otis's hit record Willie and the Hand Jive and of course made its popularity spread much later in 1978 when performed by John Travolta and Olivia Newton John in the film Grease.

The Cat's Whisker was closed down in 1958 by the police who described it as being dangerously overcrowded. Owner Peter Evans later opened the first in the chain of Angus Steak Houses at this venue. These days the building is a Korean restaurant.

Drummonds

73-77 Euston Road, Kings Cross NW1 2QS

Formerly the Euston Tavern, this pub was called Drummonds for a while and during 1988 and 1989 hosted live indie bands in a large room upstairs, a few of whom went onto greater success.

Bands who played here included Cud, Th' Faith Healers, Lush, The Wolfhounds, The Daily Planet, The Jazz Butcher, McCarthy, The Keatons, Jesus Jones, Motorcycle Boy, Television Personalities, and 14 Iced Bears. Spacemen 3 played a 'secret gig' though it was not a complete line-up as co-frontman Jason Pierce just stood at the bar during the performance.

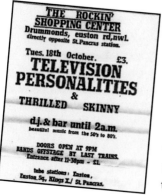

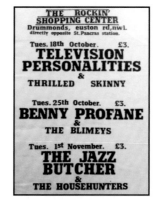

The pub is now called O'Neill's, part of an Irish-themed chain.

Embassy Night Club

7 Old Bond Street, Mayfair, W1S 4PH

29 Old Burlington Street, Mayfair, W1S 3AN

The Embassy Night Club opened in Old Bond Street in 1978 and became a fashionable hangout for people with money, inspired by clubs in New York such as Studio 54.

Early on it was frequented by David Bowie, Pete Townshend and Mick Jagger and then David Beckham, Prince Harry and Kate Moss in its later home from 2001 in Old Burlington Street. In 2013, the press reported that two Russian multimillionaires racked up a bar tab of more than £130,000 in an evening at the Embassy after competing who could rack up the highest bill. Whilst the club was better known for its sophisticated nightlife the strict dress code was relaxed on odd nights when it hosted live bands, especially during the 1980s at the old premises with several acts playing here before they were famous. Curiosity Killed the Cat made their live debut here, as did Kajagoogoo, whose singer Limahl worked at the club. The Waterboys, Sigue Sigue Sputnik, The Sisters of Mercy, Hurrah! and The Stone Roses played here too.

After moving premises, there were some live events such as a one-off reunion of original goth club Batcave here in 2009 with Specimen and Sexbeat.

The Universal and The 45s played an Amy Winehouse Foundation event and during the same years a Kings of Leon Hyde Park concert after-show party hosted live sets by The Jude and Faithful Child.

The Embassy Club closed in 2014 and was demolished soon afterwards and replaced by a block of luxury apartments. The former Old Bond Street premises are now a Dolce and Gabbana fashion shop.

Empire Rooms/Embassy Rooms

161 Tottenham Court Road, WIT 7NN

The basement of the art deco block of flats called Paramount Court has seen many uses over the years.

Originally it was the Paramount Dance Hall, renowned for its jitterbug dances during World War II, which was then renamed the Empire Rooms in the early 1950s hosting dinner dances with orchestras. By the late 1960s and early 1970s a few bands on the popular gig circuit played here including The Herd, Status Quo, Black Sabbath and Van Der Graaf Generator and then again in 1983/4 with The Redskins, The Daintees, Death Cult and Pogue Mahone all playing gigs here. As well as gigs the venue held various banqueting events, bar mitzvahs and even the 1972 International Magic Convention. Later it was renamed the Cockney Cabaret club and then in 1999, The Embassy Rooms, becoming a regular, albeit brief, haunt for gig goers. PJ Harvey, The Auteurs, James, Godspeed You! Black Emperor, ABC, Bill Wyman's Rhythm Kings, Shellac, Rufus Wainwright, Widespread Panic, Seafood, Culture Club and Levellers all played here in the Embassy Room's short existence of just a year.

Since 2000 the venue has operated as Spearmint Rhino, an American chain of strip clubs.

The End

18 West Central Street, Bloomsbury, WC1A 1JJ

This basement nightclub, partly funded by Mr C of The Shamen started in 1995 in a former mail distribution centre. This was described as one of a new era of clubs whose all-night licensing was in response to the clampdown on illegal warehouse raves. Posters were displayed across London that read: "The End is Coming".

Various musical genres were played there on different club nights including techno and house, drum and bass and breakbeat, dubstep and indie at a club night called Trash. Roni Size won the Mercury Music Prize whilst hosting a residency at the club in 1997 and the following year Fatboy Slim was resident DJ at the club whilst topping the charts.

While the venue had an esteemed reputation for DJ nights it also hosted live acts Suicide, Daft Punk and The Shamen during the late 1990s, and Ikara Colt, The Duke Spirit, Peaches, Electric Six, Death From Above, Mouse on Mars, Yeah Yeah Yeahs, Scissor Sisters, The Long Blondes, Bloc Party and Campag Velocet during the 2000s, mainly on the Trash nights. Many musicians such as the Pet Shop Boys, Kings of Leon, Muse, Marilyn Manson and The Strokes were spotted on nights out at Trash.

A developer purchased the whole island block that the club premises were located on and The End closed in 2009. Whilst the owners decided what to do with the site the venue reopened as The Den for a while but that is since closed and the club remains vacant with property guardians living on the upper floors of the building.

The Green Man/Portlands

383 Euston Road, Fitzrovia, NW1 3AU

This pub is built on the site of a tavern originally called the Farthing Pie House which was founded in 1708. In those days the tavern was noted for its live music sessions with landlord Mr Price, who was known for his skill in making music by beating a salt-box with a rolling pin, accompanied by string musicians. In 1809 it was renamed the Green Man.

bettina's 383 Euston Road, N.W.1

Thurs., 21st The nation's No. 1 rock 'n' disco.
WILD WAX SHOW 40p
Fri., 22nd A bit of R'n'B . . .
Ronnie & Bigs, Live. 60p
Sat., 23rd An exciting new jazz—rock band
Oceans. Live. 60p
Situated in the Green Man, opposite Gt. Portland Street Tube.

The cellar bar of the Green Man was called Bettina's during the mid-1970s, and held regular discos with bands playing such as Teenage Rebels, The Fabulous Poodles and Tiger Lily (who would later change their name to Ultravox). The venue was known as the Wunderbar by 1978 when UK Subs and Raped played gigs there and in 1981 under the name of The Pits it hosted gigs by Rubella Ballet, A Flock of Seagulls, The Meteors, China Crisis, Alternative TV, The Higsons, Naked Lunch and The Drones.

The pub changed its name to Portlands later in the 1980s and gigs continued in the cellar billed as the Cool Trout Basement run by the author of indie fanzine Trout Fishing in Leytonstone. Television Personalities, The Sugarcubes, Momus, The Bodines, Inspiral Carpets, The Primitives, Loop and Mega City Four all played here between 1987 and 1988. A Melody Maker review of The Primitives gig in 1988 which saw 300 people squeezed into the basement said, "the stage is no more than a ripple in the carpet....in a room that was built as a storage cupboard."

The pub reverted to the Green Man and the cellar hosted jazz sessions and more recently current owners Greene King amended the pub spelling to the Greene Man.

Hanover Grand

6 Hanover Street, Mayfair, W1S 1YZ

The Hanover Grand was previously, at various times, a Masonic hall, a restaurant and banqueting hall and the Hannover Grand Film Theatre.

The venue was vacant for ten years before reopening as a popular 900 capacity nightclub in 1995. It was so popular that Bono of U2 and Michael Hutchence of INXS were refused entry one evening as the club was too packed. As well as club nights and celebrity parties the venue hosted many gigs including low-key tour warm up shows by David Bowie in 1997 and Mike and The Mechanics in 1999.

There were also gigs by Suede, Idlewild, Republica, Starsailor, Morcheeba, Manic Street Preachers, Space, Black Grape, Lostprophets, Crowded House, Shampoo, Marc Almond and Shed Seven.

Filming for Channel 5's Pepsi Chart Show took place at the Hannover Grand where Des'ree, Alexia and B*Witched were among those performing their hits.

The Hanover Grand closed in 2002 and the former club is now a bank.

HMV Oxford Street

363 Oxford Street, W1C 2LA and 150 Oxford Street, W1D 1ND

Opened in 1921 with Sir Edward Elgar performing at the opening ceremony, this was HMV's first ever record store and, aside from the two years during the late 1930s where the building was reconstructed following fire damage, the retailer retained a presence on Oxford Street until the flagship store closed down in 2019, when the chain was bought out of administration and a rescue deal led to the closure of many UK stores.

In 1952 the store sold Britain's very first 45rpm vinyl single. HMV moved to even larger premises at 150 Oxford Street in 1986 and was advertised as the world's largest record store but it returned to its original premises in 2013 and was reopened by Sir Paul McCartney. A blue plaque celebrates the 78rpm demo disc cut by The Beatles in the store's recording studio which led to their long-term recording contract with EMI. Incidentally, another plaque of interest is at nearby 126 Piccadilly which celebrates the studio where the famous dog and-gramophone HMV trademark was painted.

From the late 1980s HMV stores hosted in-store performances and signing sessions by artists promoting their latest releases. In-store performances at 150 Oxford Street included those by The Bible, Big Country, The Boo Radleys, Stereolab, Cast, Paul Weller, Joe Strummer and The Mescaleros, Coldplay, Franz Ferdinand, Kings of Leon, Madonna, British Sea Power, Sparks, Amy Winehouse, Madness and The Streets. Blur played a rooftop gig in 1995. The following year the Spice Girls turned on the Oxford Street Christmas lights outside the store. Melanie C returned in 1997 to perform tracks from her solo album as did Emma Bunton in 2001.

In-store performances by acts at 363 Oxford Street included those by The

Horrors, Kasabian, The Vaccines, Olly Murs, Laura Marling, Kaiser Chiefs, Snow Patrol, Wolf Alice, Bullet for My Valentine, Judie Tzuke and Don Broco. HMV's former premises at number 363 is currently vacant and number 150 is now a branch of Sports Direct.

Imperial College

Prince Consort Road, South Kensington, SW7 2BB

The Concert Hall at Imperial College Union was an important gig venue from the 1960s until relatively recent years.

In 2013 ex-student Brian May unveiled a plaque commemorating Queen's first concert in London at the Union in 1970. He said that it was Queen's first ever "proper gig". He had been part of the Entertainment Committee and was influential in booking the live music which took place every Saturday. His earlier band 1984 played here in 1967 supporting Jimi Hendrix, and his later band Smile, whose members included May and Roger Taylor, played their debut gig here supporting Pink Floyd in 1968. Queen returned to play another five gigs at Imperial College between 1970 and 1973. After completing a degree in physics, May went on to study a PhD. After the launch of the Queen II album in 1974, which led to international recognition, May left the College to focus on the band but returned to gain his doctorate in Astronomy in 2007, a full 36 years after starting his thesis.

Other acts who played the college in the 1970s include Mott The Hoople, Yes, Shakin' Stevens and the Sunsets, Nazareth, Stray, Argent, Lou Reed, David Bowie, Can, Wizzard, J. Geils Band, Elton John, Family, Lindisfarne, The Sweet, Sensational Alex Harvey Band, Procol Harum, Leo Sayer, Sailor, George Melly, Gong, Flamin' Groovies, XTC and Def Leppard. Later years saw gigs by The Sisters of Mercy, Cocteau Twins, Pendragon, Mud, The Milkshakes, The Gymslips, The Higsons, New Model Army, Voice of the Beehive, Levellers and Jamiroquai. An Ian Brown show in 2011 was among the last gigs here.

The Concert Hall now concentrates on screening films and performances by the Imperial College Dramatic Society.

IMPERIAL COLLEGE
Prince Consort Road, S.W.7
Saturday, 18th October 8 p.m.
HORSLIPS
+ Jonathan Kelly
Admission £1 in advance. £1.10 on door
Saturday, 25th October **SAILOR**
Tickets available from I.C. Union Office, Prince Consort Road.
S.W.7. S.A.E. or Virgin Records, Oxford Street, W.1. Enquiries
to:- 01-589 5111, ext. 2154/2229

PRS for Music
QUEEN
first public performance
in London here
18 July 1970
PRS for Music Heritage Award

IMPERIAL COLLEGE
Prince Consort Road, London, SW.7
SATURDAY, FEBRUARY 19th, at 8 pm
IN THE GREAT HALL
SUZI QUATRO
+ SUPPORT
Tickets £1.40 in advance, available from Virgin
(London) and I.C. Ents. Enquiries: 01-589 5111 E

IC ENTS
TONIGHT! –
Tues 23 Oct – OSIBISA – Heavy Metal Kids on night
in Great Hall – 50p on night
Thurs, 25 Oct – Soldier Blue + Bob, Card. Tred 6 Alice
6.30 in Mech. Eng. 220 – 10p
Fri, 26 Oct – DISCO in Lower Refect – 50p
Sat, 27 Oct – MANFRED MANN'S EARTHBAND
in Great Hall. IC students 50p in advance
Fri, 2 Nov – QUEEN – Union Concert Hall – 30p
Sat, 3 Nov – SHAFT – 7.30 in Mech Eng 220 – 10p
FOLK SOC.
Sat, 17 Nov – RALPH McTELL – in Great Hall
IC Students 70p in advance
Tickets will be available later this week
JAZZ SOC.
Sat, 24 Nov – BACK DOOR – in Great Hall
IC Students 50p in advance
Tickets available from Nov
TICKETS FROM UNION OFFICE

MOTT THE HOOPLE
JUNKYARD ANGEL

SPRING

IMPERIAL COLLEGE, S.W.7
presents on April 25th
GENESIS
plus P.C. KENT
at 8 p.m.
Rear of Albert Hall   S.U. Cards only
01-589 2963   6/-
Next week: WILD ANGELS – LITTLE FREE ROCK

All tickets 30p   Tel. Harlow 31946
SPRING
AT IMPERIAL COLLEGE GREAT HALL
Feb. 12th   8 p.m.   Buses to Albert Hall
Exclusive Central London   Tube to South Kensington
appearance of
DAVID BOWIE
+ SUTHERLAND BROS.
Tickets advance 50p from I.C. or Virgin
Tel. 589 2963
N/W ARGENT   50p

IMPERIAL COLLEGE ENTS. PRESENTS
SHAKIN STEVENS
IN THE SUNSET
NAZARETH
8 p.m. SATURDAY NOVEMBER 20th
I.C. Union, Prince Consort Road, S.W.7
Bars ★ Disco T ★ Guerilla Lights
Tube: South Ken. ★ Bus: Albert Hall
Telephone: 01-589 2963
Also: Disco every Friday

IMPERIAL COLLEGE UNION PRESENTS
SAT. 15TH MAR.
FAMILY SMILE
PLUS SUPPORTING GROUP.
DISCO : LIC. BAR
8-00: SU CARDS ONLY
BUS TO ALBERT HALL, TUBE TO SOUTH KEN.

King's College London Students' Union

Macadam Building, Surrey Street, WC2R 2NS

The Student Union at the Strand Campus of King's College put on live acts such as Cream, Van der Graaf Generator, The Who, Stackridge and The Moody Blues in the 1960s and early 1970s in a building around the corner on the Strand.

This was until the Macadam Building opened in 1975 as the new home to the Student's Union where, in the 600-capacity main hall on the 4th floor, Adam and the Ants, Generation X, The Police, The Stranglers and Split Enz played during the late 1970s. In the 1980s the hall was known as Mandela Hall when it hosted The Smiths, Aztec Camera, A Certain Ratio and The House of Love. By 1992 the hall was renamed Tutu's after Archbishop Desmond Tutu who studied at the college during the 1960s.

The Foo Fighters made their UK debut here in 1995. Travis, Bis, Sleater Kinney, Placebo and Beck played here too in the same decade and the hall hosted the popular Collide-a-Scope indie club night at the height of Britpop.

During the 2000s many big names played here until the demise of Tutu's in 2013. These included Linkin Park, Green Day Macklemore, Vampire Weekend, Foals, The Vaccines, HAIM, and Alanis Morissette. The venue also hosted a five-night stint by Hanson and debut UK gigs by Taylor Swift and Arcade Fire.

Dwindling numbers of students attending Tutu's and financial losses brought an end to events at the Macadam Building. King's College London Students' Union is now located in nearby Bush House on The Aldwych, though it no longer hosts gigs.

Metropolis Music presents

60 FT DOLLS

plus GOLD BLADE

Friday 26th April LONDON KINGS COLLEGE

Tickets £7 any from Venue 0171 836 7132, E&C Hotline 0171 287 0932,
Stargreen 0171 937 8932, Ticketmaster 0171 344 4444 & usual agents

RIVERMAN present:

FOO FIGHTERS
+ SUPPORT
SATURDAY 3rd JUNE 1995
King's College London Students Union
Surrey Street, London, WC2R 2NS
Doors 7.00pm   £7.00 adv.
INCLUDES FREE ENTRY TO COLLIDE-A-SCOPE
AFTER SHOW
R.O.A.R. - NO READMISSION

Friday 20th January   7.30 p.m.

PREFAB SPROUT
+ THE DAINTEES
+ THE LINK MEN

Tickets £2.00 Adv.   £2.50 door

Friday 27th January   7.30 p.m.

A CERTAIN RATIO
+ SUPPORT

Tickets £3.00 Adv.   £3.50 door

Friday 3rd February   7.30 p.m.

THE CHEVALIER BROTHERS
+ INTERNATIONAL RESCUE
+ JOOLZ

Tickets £2.00 Adv.   £2.50 door

**Kings College, Macadam Building,
Surrey St, London WC2
Tel: 01-836 7132**

METROPOLIS MUSIC presents

GUIDED BY VOICES

plus Special Guests

KING'S COLLEGE STUDENTS UNION
SURREY STREET, WC2

Thursday 7th September 1995
Doors 7:00 pm
Tickets £7.00 Advance

00382

King's College London Students' Union

London School of Economics

84-86 Great Eastern Street, Shoreditch EC2A 3HY

Mick Jagger was a student here from 1961 until 1963, leaving when the Rolling Stones obtained a recording contract. The Rolling Stones never actually played a gig here but the Entertainments Committee organised gigs here for several decades.

Bands who played here in the 1960s include Chicken Shack, Tyrannosaurus Rex, Ten Years After, John Mayall and The Bluesbreakers and the Savoy Brown Blues Band. Into the 1970s there were shows by Thunderclap Newman, Wizzard, Faces, Steeleye Span, Gong, The Fall, The Pretenders and Sad Cafe. MC5 played in 1972 at the start of their European tour but without bassist Michael Davis who was detained by airport security in Detroit. Sham 69 played a riotous gig (often the case back then) resulting in £7500 damage to the venue. U2, Aztec Camera, JoBoxers, The Durutti Column, Suzanne Vega, McCarthy, Loop, The House of Love, The Charlatans and Del Amitri were among the acts to play here during the 1980s. The 1990s saw gigs by Spiritualised, Ride, Stereolab, Strangelove and Silverfish.

During the early 2000s The Cooper Temple Clause, The Long Blondes and The Futureheads played here.

Gigs eventually dried up and for the past decade live music has been limited to choirs and orchestras.

Lyceum Ballroom

Wellington Street, Covent Garden, WC2E 7RQ

The origins of the Lyceum Theatre date back to 1765 on an adjacent site. The theatre in the current location opened in 1834 though only the original facade and portico survived after a rebuild in 1904. Bram Stoker worked for 20 years as business manager of the theatre and the theatre manager Henry Irving was Stoker's real-life inspiration for the character Count Dracula in his 1897 novel.

The Theatre closed down in 1939 and was threatened with demolition, but it was saved and re-opened after the war as the Lyceum Ballroom hosting swing/dance bands. The Miss World contest was staged at the venue every year from 1951 to 1968.

From 1968 onwards the theatre was used as a pop and rock concert venue with Joe Cocker, Steppenwolf, Procol Harum, Family, Pink Floyd, Soft Machine, The Nice, The Moody Blues, The Who and The Rolling Stones playing there during the last couple of years of the decade. John Lennon made his last ever UK live appearance when the Plastic Ono Band played a benefit here along with Desmond Dekker in 1969. Eric Clapton's Derek and The Dominos played their debut gig here on June 14th 1970. Other acts to play here during the first half of the decade included Pink Fairies, Atomic Rooster, Free, T. Rex, The Kinks, Santana, Black Sabbath, Faces and the Grateful Dead, who played four nights in a row. The latter half of the 1970s saw shows by the likes of XTC, Sex Pistols, AC/DC, Madness, Queen, Toyah, The Cure, The Police, UK Subs, Motörhead, The Runaways, The Jam, Wire and Talking Heads.

Prince played his first UK gig here in 1981, and the same year The Clash played seven nights in a row with Theatre of Hate as the support band. Wham! performed for five nights in 1983 and right up to the venue's closure in 1986 there were regular concerts including those by Haircut 100, Cyndi Lauper, The Sisters of Mercy, Ramones, The Fall, Hanoi Rocks, New Model Army, The Smiths, Eurythmics, Simple Minds, Bow Wow Wow, Depeche Mode, Dead Kennedys, Ultravox, Iron Maiden and Soft Cell.

After the much-loved Lyceum closed down it lay derelict for almost a decade, but it was restored in 1996 helped by National Lottery funding and was converted back to live theatre use for large-scale musicals. It has been home to The Lion King since 1999.

Lyceum Ballroom

Paris Theatre

12 Lower Regent Street, SW1Y 4PE

The Paris Theatre was in the basement of an office building named Rex House

just south of Piccadilly Circus. Originally opened as a cinema in 1939 initially screening European (usually French) feature films, it was requisitioned by the Government during World War II and afterwards it became a radio studio for the BBC, known as the BBC Paris Studios (aka Paris Theatre). Many comedy programmes which required a live audience were broadcast live from the Paris Studios, including the radio series of Dad's Army. Its audience capacity of only 400 guests and a low stage gave an intimacy ideal for broadcasts.

In the 1960s live music sessions were recorded at the Paris Studios. The Beatles performed many studio sessions here in 1962 and 1963. From the late 1960s musical acts were often recorded in front of studio audiences as part of the In Concert and Sounds of the Seventies series. Acts to play here include Fleetwood Mac, Leonard Cohen, Faces, Soft Machine, Van der Graaf Generator, Can, Queen, AC/DC, Whitesnake, Dire Straits, Skids, Sham 69, XTC, The Style Council, Talk Talk, U2 and Bad Manners. Many of the recordings were released as official LPs, by acts such as Generation X, Curved Air, The Sensational Alex Harvey Band and John Martyn, while many ended up as bootlegs such as recordings by The Jam, Led Zeppelin, Pink Floyd and Bob Marley and the Wailers to name but a few.

The Paris Theatre was closed in 1995, being replaced by the BBC Radio Theatre in Broadcasting House. The site remained empty for many years before it was converted into its current use as a gym. Lower Regent Street was officially renamed to Regent Street St James in 2014.

Polytechnic of Central London

115 New Cavendish Street, Fitzrovia, W1W 6UW

This building, overshadowed by the British Telecom Tower, was opened in 1970 to accommodate a campus of the newly formed Polytechnic of Central London which was an amalgamation of several nearby educational establishments.

Between 1970 and 1992 the bands that played at the Student Union included Soft Machine, Electric Light Orchestra, John Martyn, The Ruts, New Order, Fuzzbox, Shop Assistants, The Bluebells, Talulah Gosh, The Stone Roses, Radiohead and The Wonder Stuff.

The Polytechnic organised many benefit gigs. In 1970 Donovan played for the World Wildlife Fund, Sham 69 and Misty in Roots played a Rock against Racism gig in 1978 and The Jam played Jobs not YOPs in 1982, an event which opposed the government's Youth Opportunities Programme. The Redskins played an anti-apartheid gig here in 1985 and a recording of this was released on CD.

In 1992 the Polytechnic of Central London was re-designated as the University of Westminster and Student Union activities were located elsewhere bringing an end to live music at New Cavendish Street.

Polytechnic of Central London S.U.
115 New Cavendish Street, W.1
Friday, October 12th at 8 pm

UNISHMENT OF
LUXURY
+ The Resistance
Admission £1.40 N.U.S., £1.60 Others

POLYTECHNIC OF CENTRAL LONDON
115 Cavendish Street W.1

FRIDAY DECEMBER 7th 7.30 pm to 12 pm

*Benefit For Rock Against Sexism/
National Abortion Campaign*

GIRLSCHOOL
PATRIK FITZGERALD
AU PAIRS
THE MISSTAKES

Admission: £1.50 NUS/Unwaged £2 Others
Nearest Tube Goodge Street, Oxford Circus

Poly Of Central London S.U.
presents

HE MONOCHROME SET
+
ZERRA 1
Friday 8th October 8pm
115 New Cavendish St, W1
£2.00 Students — Unwaged £2.50 Others
Tickets from S.U. 01-636 6271

PCLSU *presents a No Nukes Benefit*

DOLL BY DOLL
AU PAIRS

THIS HEAT
FLATBACKERS

Friday 24th October, 7.30 till late — Bar

POLY OF CENTRAL LONDON
115 NEW CAVENDISH ST., W1
(Oxford Circus Tube)

Tickets £2.00 (Students £1.80, unwaged £1)
Advance 636 6271

115
New Cavendish Street

Princess Louise

208 High Holborn, Holborn, WC1V 7EP

An upstairs room of this pub built in 1872 was home to the Ballads and Blues Club from the mid-1950s, founded by folk singer Ewan MacColl and others. The club was named after Ewan MacColl's BBC radio programme of the same name.

The Ballads and Blues Club was one of the earliest English folk clubs. Before, there were two skiffle clubs which met in the Princess Louise, which included folk singers among the musicians. Performers of the Ballads and Blues Club included Ewan MacColl, Peggy Seeger, Seamus Ennis, Fitzroy Coleman, Dominic Behan, Stan Kelly and Isla Cameron. An audience committee ruled that performers should sing in a language that you could speak and understand and not sing the same traditional song more than once every three months after they became tired of hearing the same songs week after week. During this period MacColl wrote The First Time Ever I Saw Your Face which became one of his best-known songs.

By 1958 The Ballads and Blues Club moved on to a succession of venues around London. In 1961 MacColl and Seeger started the breakaway Singers Club around London pubs returning to the Princess Louise in 1977, the same year that they got married. MacColl's daughter from a previous marriage was the singer Kirsty MacColl.

The pub continues to trade and its preserved Victorian interior noted for the marble urinals in the gent's toilets resulted in Historic England awarding it Grade II listed building status.

Regent Street Polytechnic

4–12 Little Titchfield Street, Fitzrovia, W1W 7BY

This building where the gigs took place was an annexe of the main 309 Regent Street campus. During the second half of the

1960s the Student Union organised gigs here by The Move, Howlin' Wolf, The Who, Black Sabbath, Fleetwood Mac, Cream, The Action, Soft Machine, Manfred Mann, John Mayall's Bluesbreakers and Brian Auger and The Trinity. Hype, whose line-up included David Bowie, Mick Ronson and Tony Visconti, played a gig here in early 1970.

The Regent Street building has a Pink Floyd plaque which was unveiled by Nick Mason and Roger Waters in 2015 to celebrate the band's 50th anniversary. The pair, together with Richard Wright, formed the group while studying architecture at the university. They rehearsed at Little Titchfield Street, initially as Sigma 6, and

played gigs here as the Tea Set in 1964 and 1965. By this time, Syd Barrett had joined the group as frontman. Being a fan of both Pink Anderson and Floyd Council, he combined the names to make Pink Floyd Sound, which would be later shorted to Pink Floyd. They played gigs here in 1967 and 1968.

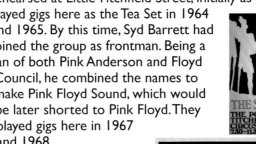

In 1970, the Regent Street Polytechnic merged with other colleges and became the Polytechnic of Central London (now the University of Westminster) and live music events were relocated to a new building on New Cavendish Street.

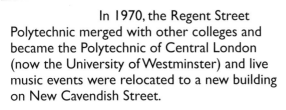

53

Revolution

14-16 Bruton Place, Mayfair, W1J 6LX

The Revolution club opened in 1968 at premises previously called Le Prince club and was owned, along with Blaises and The Speakeasy (see volume 1 of London's Lost Music Venues), by Iraqi businessman David Shamoon. As with his other clubs, Revolution was aimed at upmarket people who liked to rub shoulders with famous musicians and people in the fashion industry.

The club with an audience capacity of around 100 guests hosted live acts most nights. Cream played here and part of their gig was recorded for a French TV Show with live tracks later to surface on their Transmissions LP. Yes played here six times and other acts who played here include Genesis, Chicago, Patti LaBelle And The Bluebells, Kenny Rogers and the First Edition, Deep Purple, Elton John, Gene Vincent, Joni Mitchell, King Crimson, Ambrose Slade and Timebox. Smile played here in 1969, a year before changing their name to Queen. Grateful Dead were advertised to here to play here in 1968 but the tour was cancelled and the band never got to play Europe until 1972 when they played two dates at the much larger Empire Pool (now known as Wembley Arena).

1969 JUNE dates	Blaises	Revolution	Speakeasy
SUN 1	Sarolta		
MON 2	Methuseleah	KING CRIMSON	Spirit of John Morgan
TUE 3	Ambrose Slade	MARBLES/Majority	Samson-
WED 4	Majority	Root & Jenny Jackson	Glass Menagerie
THUR 5	Jo Jo Gunn	Interstate Road Show	KEITH RELF's Renaissance
FRI 6	Blonde on Blonde	Flames	Velvet Opera
SAT 7	Exception	Arcadium	Audience

DJ Tony Blackburn's television programme Time for Blackburn featured clips from the Revolution in 1968. The club hosted a fashion show the same year with George Harrison's wife Pattie as one of the models. The show was attended by her husband and fellow Beatle John Lennon as well as Elizabeth Taylor and Richard Burton.

The live music stopped in 1971 and the former club is currently a Michelin Star Restaurant called Umu.

REVOLUTION

1969 dates	Blaises	Revolution
1	Sarolta	
2	Methuselah	KING CRIMSON
3	Ambrose Slade	MARBLES/Majority
4	Majority	Root & Jenny Jackson
R 5	Jo Jo Gunn	Interstate Road Show
6	Blonde on Blonde	Flames
7	Exception	Arcadium
8	Root & Jenny Jackson	
9	Entire Sioux Nation	KING CRIMSON
10	Flames	3 DOG NIGHT/SOJM
11	East of Eden	Jo Jo Gunn
12	Spirit of John Morgan	Ohio Express/Majority
13	Black Velvet	Circus
14		
15	Ferris Wheel	
N 16	Soul Committee	Samson
17	Springfield Park	CHRIS BARBER
18	Village	TERRY REID
19	Samson	Wallace Collection
20	Majority	Ski - Boo
21		Heaven
22	Fri-Boo	
23	Spirit of John Morgan	Springfield Park
24	Brainbox	The Web
25	Majority	Spirit of John Morgan
26	The Web	Sarolta
27	Procession	Flames
28		
29	Flames	
30	Clouds	Majority

	WEEK ONE	WEEK TWO	WEEK THREE	WEEK FOUR	WEEK FIVE
Mon:	30 Greatest Show on Earth.	7 Idle Race.	14 Ray King Soul	21 Majority.	28 Web.
Tues:	1 Majority.	8 Cuby & the Blizzards.	15 JOOLS DRISCOLL & BRIAN AUGER	22 LUCAS & MIKE COTTON SOUND.	29 Tuesday's Children.
Wed:	2 Sleepy.	9 Circus.	16 Majority	23 Junior's Conquest.	30 Capitol System.
Thurs:	3 O'HARA'S PLAYBOYS.	10 GRATEFUL DEAD.	17 Web	24 Time Box.	31 O'HARA'S PLAYBOYS.
Fri:	4 Freedom.	11 Mr. Mo's Messengers.	18 Aston Gardner & Dyke	25 Mr. Mo's Messengers.	1
Sat:	5 Affinity.	12	19	26 Tages.	2

14-16 Bruton Place, Berkeley Square, London W1 Reservations 01-629 6264/7, 01-695 2517

The Roaring Twenties Club (and many others)

50 Carnaby Street, Soho, W1F 9QA

The basement of this address was the site of several live music venues.

From 1936, the site was the Florence Mills Social Parlour, a combination of a restaurant, social centre and jazz club formed by political activist Marcus Garvey and calypso singer Sam Manning.

In the 1940s it was the Blue Lagoon Club, allegedly a front for prostitution. In 1946, Margaret Cook, an exotic dancer was shot dead in the narrow alleyway outside the club. During 2015, a 91-year-old man living in a care home confessed to the shooting which would make this the longest gap between a crime and a confession in British criminal history.

In the 1950s it was initially Club Eleven, a jazz club founded by Ronnie Scott and ten other musicians (hence the club's name), which was closed down following by a police raid for drugs after only six months. It then became the Sunset Club, an all-night jazz and calypso club particularly frequented by American GIs. The Russ Henderson Steel Band, the first steel band in Britain, played their first ever gig there. Trinidadian Rupert Nurse became a bandleader at the house which became one of the top venues for Caribbean music in London in the 1950s, although that didn't prevent it from going bankrupt in 1959.

The Roaring Twenties opened in 1962 and Jamaican born Count Suckle became resident DJ and bouncer with many of his followers attending. It had a reputation as a place for Caribbean people and mods to dance to the latest imports of rhythm and blues, soul, and bluebeat/ska. The Rolling Stones, The Animals and The Who came to the club, and according to Suckle, a 17-year-old

Mick Jagger would borrow the records that Suckle ordered by post from a shop in Tennessee, rehearse them and bring them back. Cyril Davies All-Stars played a residency in 1963 and Georgie Fame and the Blue Flames played here numerous times the same year. Suckle moved off to run the Cue Club but the Roaring Twenties continued for a few years after he left. Other acts to play over the next few years included Edwin Starr, The Original Drifters, The Links, The Coloured Raisins, Joe E Young and The Toniks and Cats Pyjamas.

The club changed its name to Columbo's in the early 1970s, and Bob Marley and his entourage would party there after Lyceum gigs in 1975. Columbo's closed in the early 1980s, later becoming a dance club called Ruby's until the 1990s.

Today, the basement serves as part of a retail unit.

Royalty Theatre

Portugal Street, Holborn, WC2A 2HT

The Royalty was originally a small theatre situated on Dean Street in Soho, which opened in 1840 as Miss Kelly's Theatre and Dramatic School. It closed to the public in 1938 and was demolished in 1953. A modern Royalty Theatre was opened in the basement of a newly constructed office block at Portugal Street in 1960 on the site of the former London Opera House.

After initially hosting a few plays the 1,000 capacity Royalty was used as a cinema screening Cinerama films for most of the 1960s but by 1970 returned to live theatre use. During the 1970s porn baron Paul Raymond held The Great International Nude Show revue here, a show which involved two dolphins that were kept in a massive tank beneath the stage. During the shows, the tanks would be raised up to the stage and the dolphins would swim around, do some tricks and ultimately remove the bikini from Miss Nude International. Urban legend has it that the dolphins died from neglect and the Theatre is haunted by the dolphins, though in reality at the end of the show's run the animals were moved to a dolphinarium in East Asia.

In 1974 The Kinks performed their Preservation stage musical here for three nights. Alan Price played a concert here in 1975 followed by several jazz acts that year including Sammy Rimington, Barry Martyn and The Louisiana Shakers. Gigs in 1977 were advertised as 'Sound Circus at the Royalty Theatre' when Scorpions played for two nights on their Virgin Killer Tour. There were also gigs by Can, Tom Waits and one of the last ever live performances by Sandy Denny from Fairport Convention who passed away the following year. This performance was recorded and released as her live album, Gold Dust. Joy Division played here at the end of the decade.

During the 1980s the Royalty was used as a TV studio for ITV's This is Your Life and gigs were few and far between although Peter Hammill, Marc Almond, Elvis

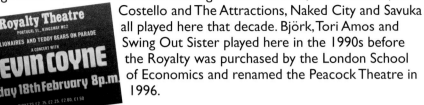

Costello and The Attractions, Naked City and Savuka all played here that decade. Björk, Tori Amos and Swing Out Sister played here in the 1990s before the Royalty was purchased by the London School of Economics and renamed the Peacock Theatre in 1996.

The Peacock is a lecture hall by day and a venue for the Sadler's Wells Theatre company by night.

Saville Theatre

135 Shaftesbury Avenue, Covent Garden, WC2H 8AH

The 1,400 capacity Saville Theatre opened in 1931. From 1963, a musical adaption of the Pickwick Papers featuring Harry Secombe's first musical role, was a huge success and saw 694 performances at the Saville and gave Secombe the chart hit If I Ruled the World.

Brian Epstein, manager of The Beatles, leased the theatre in 1965, presenting plays and from 1966, rock and roll shows. The venue became noted for its Sunday night concerts. During one by Chuck Berry, members of the audience stormed the stage, smashed seats and slashed curtains resulting in the police attending to clear the theatre. Epstein died during the summer of 1967 but live shows continued until the Saville was sold, later to become a cinema.

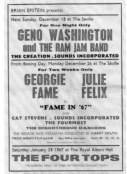

The Beatles used the Theatre for rehearsals before embarking on their 1965 US stadium tour and returned in 1967 to record the video for Hello, Goodbye. At a show there in 1967 Jimi Hendrix played Sgt. Pepper's Lonely Hearts Club Band when an impressed Paul McCartney was in the audience. The Bee Gees and Fats Domino made their UK debuts here playing on the same bill for five nights in 1967 along with Gerry and The Pacemakers.
The Bee Gees returned to the Saville later that year supported by the Bonzo Dog Doo Dah Band and The Flowerpot Men. Other acts who played the theatre include The Four Tops, Little Richard, Cream, The Who, Pink Floyd, Jeff Beck Group, Ben E King, Bo Diddley, Manfred Mann, Fairport Convention and The Crazy World of Arthur Brown. The Rolling Stones played two shows the same evening here in December 1969 and became the last ever band to play the Saville.

Following a short run of a play starring Dennis Waterman, the theatre, which by now had been taken over by EMI was converted to a two-screen cinema in 1970. The stage area became administration offices and now little of the original theatre internal structure remains.

In 2001 the building was taken over again, and it is now the four-screen Odeon Covent Garden cinema.

Saint Martin's School of Art

107 Charing Cross Road, Soho, WC2H 0EB

Saint Martin's School of Art was an art college that moved to this purpose-built site in 1939. Many musicians have studied at the college including Glen Matlock, Sade, Billy Childish and members of Bonzo Dog Band, X Ray Spex and The Belle Stars.

The college did not host much live music though Wishbone Ash, Glencoe, Assagai and the Ottawa Music Company (with Henry Cow) all played here in the early 1970s. The most infamous performance here was in 1975 when the Sex Pistols played their first ever gig. They carried their gear from their digs/studio over the road in Denmark Street and played for a few songs before the sound was pulled by the social secretary. That night the band were supporting Bazooka Joe who featured bass player Stuart Goddard. He would later change his name to Adam Ant.

In 2005 the college hosted a party celebrating the 30th anniversary of the Sex Pistols debut. The Paddingtons (with Glen Matlock guesting), Art Brut and Comanechi all performed at the event. In 2011, just before relocating to new premises, the college hosted a farewell party with Pulp playing a short set. Jarvis Cocker was an ex-student and Pulp name checked St Martin's College in their 1995 hit Common People. The guest DJs included Corinne Drewery of Swing Out Sister who was also an ex St Martins student.

The college now known as Central Saint Martins is currently located in a converted warehouse complex at King's Cross.

The old building is now a Foyles bookshop with The Saint Martins Lofts residential apartments situated above.

Saint Martin's School of Art

Turnmills

63 Clerkenwell Road, Clerkenwell, EC1M 5NP

This building on the corner of Clerkenwell Road and Turnmill Street started life as a warehouse and stables built in 1886 by the Great Northern Railway Company. The name 'Turnmill' originates from when the site was originally a mill beside the now subterranean River Fleet.

The building became a bar and a 1,000-people capacity nightclub in 1990. Turnmills was the first venue in the UK to get a 24-hour dance licence and became the home of several successful club nights including Trade, The Gallery and Heavenly Social. Paul Oakenfold, Judge Jules, Paul van Dyk , Roger Sanchez and Frankie Knuckles were some of the acclaimed DJs who

appeared here. Whilst best known for pre-recorded music Turnmills hosted some live acts, especially on Get Loaded nights at which Shaun Ryder from the Happy Mondays made a number of DJ appearances. Get Loaded also had live performances by The Cuban Brothers, Deaf Stereo, Metro Riots, The Casuals, El Presidente, Happy Attack, The Fades and Blood Red Bird. Together club nights also hosted bands including Thee Earls, Kids in Tracksuits, The Whip and The Metros. Bands to have played on other nights include Babyshambles, The Kills, 65daysofstatic and Queenadreena.

Turnmills attracted pop stars such as Bono, Sting, Madonna, Donna Summer and Robbie Williams to party there and Michael Jackson held his 30th birthday do there after the UK leg of his Bad tour. The place wasn't always without problems - gangster 'Mad' Frankie Fraser was shot outside the club in 1991, and in 2003 a gang forced their way into the club ahead of a performance by Lisa

Maffia of So Solid Crew. One man suffered bullet wounds inside the club and another was killed outside.

The club's lease expired in 2008 resulting in closure with Fatboy Slim and former resident DJs The Chemical Brothers on the decks for the closing

weekend. The building was subsequently demolished and a new block containing offices has been built on the site.

Turnmills in January 2008, before being demolished (courtesy of Wiki)

Virgin Megastore/Zavvi

14-16, Oxford Street, W1D 1AR

GREEN DAY

Performing LIVE
at The Virgin Megastore
14-16 Oxford Street, London

Sunday 17th September
Doors open: 10.30pm
Performance starts: 11pm

Followed by signing of new
single 'Minority'

The first Virgin Record Shop was opened by Richard Branson at 24 Oxford Street in 1971. In 1979 Virgin opened their first Megastore at the intersection of Oxford Street and Tottenham Court Road with entrances to the store on both streets. The building was originally a Lyon's Corner House food hall and restaurant built on the site of the former Oxford Music Hall / Theatre.

From the late 1980s the Megastore hosted in-store performances and signing sessions by artists to promote their latest releases. The performances took place on a stage in the basement where the musical instrument department was located. Acts that performed included The Lemonheads, Lush, Nick Cave, Bruce Dickinson, Oasis, Hole, Brian May, Carter the Unstoppable Sex Machine, The Wedding Present, Green Day, Mercury Rev, PJ Harvey, John Otway, Biffy Clyro, Tricky, My Chemical Romance, Belle and Sebastian and Ash.

In 2007, the Virgin Megastores brand broke away from the Virgin Group and the new ownership renamed all the UK stores Zavvi who became the UK's largest independent entertainment retailer. The Charlatans, Katy Perry, Keane, Biffy Clyro and Chaka Khan played there during that short era until Zavvi went into administration following the collapse of Woolworths, who owned Zavvi's supplier Entertainment UK. Zavvi was left without stock during the busy 2008 Christmas period and Zavvi Oxford Street closed in 2009. The premises are now a Primark clothing store.

EAST

333 Club

333 Old Street, Hackney, EC1V 9LE

This was originally The London Apprentice pub built in 1895. During the 1970s the London Apprentice was a popular gay pub and in 1983 it hosted the first ever Terence Higgins Trust meeting to spread awareness of AIDS.

The pub changed its image and was renamed as the 333 Club in 1998 providing a club with DJs in the main ground floor area and a room upstairs called the Mother Bar which sometimes presented live bands.

The 333 Basement club, later renamed the Hoxton Cell, also hosted live music. Acts that performed either in the basement or upstairs included Babyshambles, Arcane Roots, The Libertines, Razorlight, Pulp, Rialto, Dee Dee Ramone, Zodiac Mindwarp and the Love Reaction, The Tuts, Frank Chickens and Coldcut. The Shoreditch Twat fanzine was published for a few years as an events listing periodical for the 333 Club and a tongue-in-cheek observation of the creative boom in the area.

Live music ceased around 2013 and the venue closed down in 2019 due to licensing issues and is currently vacant.

ABC/Ritz Cinema

180 South Street, Romford, RM1 1TR

This was a 2,000 capacity cinema that opened as the Ritz in 1938. Billy Fury, Wee Willie Harris and Cliff Richard and The Shadows all played gigs here in the late 1950s and early 1960s.

In 1962 the cinema was re-named the ABC and as well as showing films hosted live music shows, often two performances by each act per evening. Acts to play included The Hollies, Small Faces, The Nashville Teens, Gene Pitney, Roy Orbison, Jeff Beck Group, The Settlers and The Kinks. The Beatles played here early in 1963 performing a six-song set as part of a package tour with Tommy Roe, The Viscounts, Debbie Lee and the Terry Young Six. Ringo Starr's step-grandparents lived around the corner, and it has been said that the band visited them after their gig. In 1965 the Rolling Stones, who were at the time number one in the charts with their double A-side 'Play with Fire' and 'The Last Time', were returning from playing at the ABC and stopped off at a petrol station on the Romford Road in Forest Gate when Bill Wyman reportedly offended the attendant by asking, "Where can we have a leak here?" There were no toilet facilities and after asking once again Mick Jagger allegedly quipped: "We'll piss anywhere, man" prompting some of his fellow band to repeat that line in a chant while relieving themselves against the wall. After being summoned to court Wyman, Jagger and Brian Jones were all found guilty of using insulting behaviour and were each fined five pounds.

The ABC closed in 1999, was demolished the next year and replaced with flats.

ABC/Ritz Cinema

72

Albemarle Youth Club

Gooshays Drive, Harold Hill, Romford RM3 9LB

In 1960 The Albemarle Report was released, a government report which outlined the need for local government agencies to take on responsibility for providing activities for young people. This youth club just outside Romford was named after the report and built in 1963. As well as other activities it held a number of gigs until the late 1970s featuring both local and up-and-coming touring bands.

The roll call of bands that played here include Black Sabbath, Babe Ruth, Man, Hawkwind, Spinning Wheel, Kilburn and the High Roads, Judas Priest, Budgie, The Sweet, Scorpions and The Wasps. A concert in 1972 brought tragedy to the Albemarle drawing the attention of the national media when the band Storm, one of five acts playing that day, brought along a home-made cannon designed to emit smoke and sweets into the audience. Outside in the car park the band's roadie was testing out the cannon using a mixture of sugar and weed killer as explosive with a taper made of string soaked in wax. The cannon burst, killing him and seriously injuring a few others as well as blowing out the windows of the club and vehicles in the car park.

The Albemarle was closed in 2012, then demolished and replaced with a housing development.

ALBEMARLE CLUB

Gooshays Drive, Harold Hill, Romford
(Nearest Station: Harold Wood)

Friday
25th February

PAHANA

8 p.m.

30p

ALBEMARLE CLUB

Gooshays Drive, Harold Hill
Romford
(nearest station Harold Wood)

Friday, January 28th

HOG

8 p.m.   25p

Sunday, January 30th

GYPSY
RAMROD

35p   7.30

ALBEMARLE CLUB

Gooshays Drive, Harold Hill, Romford
(Nearest Station: Harold Wood)

Friday, April 21st

BLAZER

8 p.m.   30p

Sunday, April 23rd

SKIN ALLEY

7.30 p.m.   40p

Albemarle Youth Club

The Bitter End/The Horn

15 High Street, Romford, RM1 1JU

An inn on this site dates back to the 15th century that was rebuilt during Victorian times known as the White Hart Hotel which subsequently underwent many name changes.

In 2006 and 2007 when called The Bitter End it hosted acts including Towers of London, Sonic Boom Six, Chas & Dave, Napalm Death, Architects and Mystery Jets. In 2010 the pub was renamed The Horn after the team behind The Horn in St Albans briefly took it over and put on gigs by Beki Bondage, Captain Sensible, The Glitter Band, Anti Nowhere League, Eastfield and The Duel plus a few nights of tribute bands to the likes of Guns 'n' Roses and Metallica. By 2011 the pub reverted to The Bitter End continuing with many tribute bands plus an array of older long-established bands popular in their respected genres such as UK Subs, The Members, The Queers, English Dogs and Discharge for the punks, The Lambrettas for the mods and Condemned 84, The Last Resort and Close Shave for the Oi! skinheads. Later that year the live music stopped and the pub closed in 2012.

JULY @BITTER END ROMFORD
High Street Romford WWW.TBER.CO.UK

fri 1st - Bad Behaviour (rock covers) £3
sat 2nd - **RAGE AGAINST THE MACHINE** tribute £5
thu 7th - No More Heros (covers) free
fri 8th - **BERMONDSEY JOYRIDERS**   coming soon
sat 9th - U2 tribute £5
thu 14th - STORM (rock covers) free   **BANDS on SUNDAYS**
fri 15th - **NIRVANA** tribute £5
sat 16th - **GUNS & ROSES** tribute £5   check our
thu 21st - Andy Robinson Band (rock/blues) free
fri 22nd - **SHAM 69** PUNK SPECIAL   web site
sat 23rd - TBC
thu 28th - **PUNK SPECIAL**   for whats on
fri 29th - **STRANGLERS** tribute £5
sat 30th - **CREAM** tribute £5   **WWW.TBER.CO.UK**

In 2015 the empty building suffered a fire and in 2017 a group of squatters moved in who spent the next two years as self-appointed caretakers, renovating the premises with the intention of reopening it for community use. Despite much internal restoration having taken place the squatters were evicted in 2019 and the future of the empty building remains uncertain.

Cabot Hall

Cabot Place West, Canary Wharf, E14 5AB

Cabot Hall, originally intended as retail space, was opened in 1991 on the Canary Wharf Development on the Isle of Dogs as a banqueting and performance hall for regular concerts and events capable of occupying 400 people.

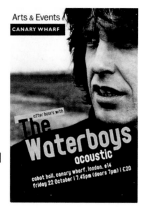

Most of the audiences were seated and the acts performed mainly acoustic sets here. These included

Judie Tzuke, The Stranglers, Alabama 3, The Wonder Stuff, Lloyd Cole, Heather Nova, Nick Harper, Glenn Tilbrook, The Waterboys, Belinda Carlisle, Eddi Reader and Dave Edmunds. Scenes from the Fat Slags film, based on the Viz comic characters of the same name, were filmed at Cabot Hall.

The Hall, as it was never originally planned to be a hall, had no backstage, an insufficient foyer space and inadequate loading facilities. In 2006 it closed down and has since been converted into a shopping mall. A smaller function hall upstairs has been turned into a high-class restaurant called Boisdale offering a supper club experience with live jazz, blues and soul curated by Jools Holland, their patron of music.

Four Aces Club/Labyrinth

12 Dalston Lane, Dalston E8 3GP

This was built as the Dalston Theatre in 1898 which retained part of a previous circus building of 1886 which was always used as the main entrance to this site until the whole building's demolition in 2007. The building was redesigned as a cinema which opened in 1920 with seating for over 2,000 people until its closure in 1960.

In 1966 the Four Aces Club, named after a then popular cigarette brand, was set up here by Jamaican immigrant Newton Dunbar, to provide a music venue catering for people from the West Indies. Dunbar showcased up-and-coming artists and later hosted legendary sound clashes and sound systems such as Count Shelly, Jah Shaka and Sir Coxsone. Live acts who played here included Jimmy Ruffin, Prince Buster, Jimmy Cliff, The Ronettes, Percy Sledge, Desmond Dekker, Ben E. King, The Upsetters, The Pioneers, Billy Ocean, Otis Redding and Stevie Wonder. The club became a hangout for a wider audience which over the years was visited by Bob Dylan, The Slits, Bob Marley and Mick Jagger. The Four Aces was often referred to as "the jewel in Dalston's crown" during the 1960s and 1970s.

During the early 1990s, the club became Labyrinth, one of the first legal indoor rave venues initially playing acid house and hardcore. The Prodigy made their first live appearance at Labyrinth which continued as a successful club until closing in 1997 after being repossessed by the local Council who had other ideas for the site.

After an unsuccessful campaign asking for the building to be preserved and a period when it was occupied by squatters it was demolished and a new development mainly of apartments was built on the site. The four towers are named Labyrinth Tower, Wonder House, Marley House and Dunbar Tower. Apparently, Newton Dunbar, who is unhappy with the gentrification of the area, said that he was not consulted about his name being used in the naming of the development.

Bunnie Lee Stars Show
To be held at the
FOUR ACES CLUB
12. DALSTON LANE, LONDON. E.8
ON
SUNDAY, 2nd DECEMBER, '73
From 8 p.m. until 5 a.m.
★ LIVE ON STAGE, DIRECT FROM JAMAICA ★
DERRICK MORGAN
moon hop   don't blame the moon   and many more hits

LLOYD **CHARMERS**	THE **GREYHOUND**

☆ and Steve Barnard Disco ☆
SOUNDS BY
COUNT SHELLY and LORD KOOS
plus other
guest Artists   ADM. £1.00

FOUR ACES ROOTS CLUB
12 DALSTON LANE, LONDON, E.8
PRESENT
THE FANTASTIC
EQUATORS
Plus ★ SIR COXONE
Meets ★ JA SHAKA
Sunday 23rd October
Sunday 30th October
Live on Stage
★ PRINCE JAZBO and
★ SIR COXONE meets
★ LORD DAVID
CLUB OPENS 7 NIGHTS
ROOTS ATMOSPHERE

Club FOUR Aces
12, DALSTON LANE, E.8
6 NIGHTS A WEEK
COUNT SHELLY
8 PM - 4 AM EVERY TUES
LADIES FREE
FRIDAY NIGHTS
SOUL GROUP COUNT SHELLY
SAT. NIGHT • Cabaret
PLEASE APPLY FOR MEMBERSHIP

****
SCOM ENTERTAINMENT
PRESENTS
*Every Wednesday
Night*
AT THE
FOUR ACES CLUB
DALSTON LANE, DALSTON E6
****

LABYRINTH
10PM TILL MORNING

LABYRINTH
EST. 1988 THE 9TH YEAR DAWNS

Granada East Ham

281 Barking Road, East Ham, E6 1LB

The Granada Theatre opened as a cinema in 1936 with 2,400 seats. In common with other Granada Theatres, it was fully equipped to stage shows as well as films.

After the second world war the Granada hosted variety shows and by the late 1950s rock 'n' roll acts including Buddy Holly and The Crickets in 1958. The 1960s saw the venue host package tours featuring acts such as Chris Montez, Percy Sledge, Stevie Wonder, Manfred Mann, The Yardbirds, Duane Eddy, Marty Wilde, Wayne Fontana and The Mindbenders, The Rolling Stones, Freddie and The Dreamers, Roy Orbison and Desmond Dekker. In 1962 the Everly Brothers started their UK tour here, but Don was hospitalised and Phil was forced to perform the show solo. The Beatles played here in 1963 and just before going onstage the band learnt that their forthcoming single, 'I Want to Hold Your Hand' was likely to have more than one million advance sales ahead of its release. Apparently the scenes outside the venue were so chaotic that a food delivery had to be accompanied by a police escort to make it through the crowds of fans.

The Granada continued to put on concerts as well as films, pantomimes and wrestling into the 1970s with concerts by Gene Pitney, Faces, Black Sabbath, Peter Frampton and Badfinger. David Essex played in 1974 the week before the cinema ceased showing films and fittingly the last film to be shown was That'll Be the Day starring David Essex. The venue continued to put on concerts. Status Quo, Mick Ronson and Hawkwind all played before The Granada became a bingo club in 1976.

The bingo stopped in 2014 and the building is now a fitness centre named Flipout which is London's biggest trampoline and adventure park.

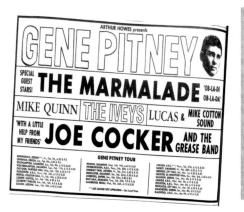

Granada Walthamstow

186 Hoe Street, Walthamstow, E17 4QS

The Granada Theatre, famed for having been frequented by Alfred Hitchcock, opened as a cinema in 1930 with almost 2,700 seats. In common with other Granada Theatres it was fully equipped to stage shows as well as films.

The Ink Spots played here in 1949 and the 1950s saw performances by Frank Sinatra, Count Basie, Des O'Connor, The Crickets, and Cliff Richard and The Shadows. The Beatles, Gene Vincent, The Kinks and The Who all played here several times during the 1960s, often as part of package tours featuring two shows per evening. In 1966 James Brown made his UK debut here. Other other notable acts to play here that decade included Gerry and The Pacemakers, Tommy Steele, Little Richard, Del Shannon, The Yardbirds, The Bryds, Marmalade, Traffic, The Tremeloes and The Dubliners. The early 1970s saw performances by Roy Orbison, Jerry Lee Lewis, Gene Pitney, Atomic Rooster and Marvin, Welch and Farrar before the Granada was divided up into a multi-screen cinema.

The cinema was later renamed the Cannon, then the ABC and finally the EMD before closure in 2003. The building was sold to a religious organisation who were unable to obtain planning permission to use the Grade II listed building. Meanwhile the building remained derelict until being bought by a pub chain who reopened the foyer as Mirth, Marvel and Maud in 2015. They hosted many live events with performances by Pye Corner Audio, Mungo Jerry, Jah Wobble and The Invaders of The Heart, John Otway, Thee Hypnotics, Laetitia Sadier Source Ensemble, David Gedge and Ren Harvieu. The pub closed in early 2020 after the building was purchased by the council as part of a £25million redevelopment project to transform it into a 1,000-seat comedy and entertainment venue. Hopefully there will be a return for live music.

Green Gate

228/230 Bethnal Green Road, Bethnal Green, E2 0AA

This pub once frequented by the infamous Kray Twins had a large room with discos and live music. The Iveys, later to find success as Badfinger, played here in the 1960s as did pianist Lennie Peters (later to top the charts as one half of Peters and Lee), who launched his career here. The venue also hosted early gigs by Tex Withers and Suzi Quatro, along with regular performances by pub circuit entertainers Brian "Butch" Royal and the Rondell Trio.

By the 1980s pub rock bands such as Eddie and the Hot Rods were playing here along with heavier rock/metal bands including Berlyn, Desolation Angels, Tredegar, No Sweat, Tilt and Sacrilege . Along with the Ruskin Arms in East Ham, it became an important venue for up-and-coming metal bands. Right up to the closure in 1995 the pub continued to put on live acts though this consisted mainly of exotic dancers and middle-of-the-road covers bands.

The premises are now used for retail. A piece of the pub sign remains on the building from its final years when the name Green Gate was reduced to just one word.

Ilford Palais/Tiffany's

Ilford Palais/Tiffany's

246-250 High Road, Ilford, IG1 1QF

This venue originally opened as the 1,000 seat Premier Electric Theatre cinema in 1911. It was later purchased by Mecca Dancing Ltd who changed its name in 1925 to the Palais De Dance, where the top dance bands of the day would play.

TV and radio presenter Jimmy Savile was the manager here between 1955 and 1956 around the same time future heavyweight boxer Billy Walker was a bouncer and a part-time DJ here. Local singer Kathy Kirby turned professional after joining bandleader Bert Ambrose onstage one night at the Ilford Palais in 1956. Ambrose took her on the club circuit, and she went on to represent the UK in the Eurovision Song Contest in 1965, coming second to the Luxembourg entry. She was perhaps overshadowed by Sandy Shaw from nearby Dagenham, who had an early break when she came second in the Ilford Palais talent contest early in the decade. She would go on to win the Eurovision Song Contest for the UK in 1967 with 'Puppet on a String'. Brian Poole And The Tremeloes played their debut live gig at the Ilford Palais in 1960. Other live acts to perform here included Bill Haley and The Comets, The Kinks, The Troggs, The Who, Small Faces, Desmond Dekker and Edwin Starr.

By the 1970s the venue was a disco called Tiffany's which occasionally had live gigs by John Martyn, Frogmorton, Barclay James Harvest, The Sweet, KC and The Sunshine Band and The Tourists. Level 42 played there in 1982 before the name reverted to the Palais when a number of mod revival all-dayers were held where acts such as The Truth, Purple Hearts, Squire and Mari Wilson performed live sets. Later it became a nightclub named Fifth Avenue, and finally Jumpin' Jacks.

The promotional music video for 'Come Dancing' by The Kinks was shot at Ilford Palais in 1982.

The building met a similar fate to that of the Palais described in the lyrics of the song after it was demolished in 2007 after having been derelict for several years. A high-rise block of flats called Raphael House now stands on the site.

The Island

300-310 High Road, Ilford, IG1 1QW

This venue originally opened in 1937 as The Regal Cinema and was re-named the ABC in 1973. It closed as a cinema in 1984 before being converted into the Granada Bingo club.

Bingo ceased here in 1989 and the venue eventually reopened in 1992 as a 1,700 capacity nightclub called The Island, hosting regular rave nights and an indie/alternative rock night initially called

Alcatraz and then Supersonic mainly with DJs though guest live bands such as Bis, Dweeb, Hurricane #1 and Symposium would occasionally play. Concerts were also hosted at The Island with Babybird, Feeder, Mansun, Sleeper, Oasis, The Prodigy, Mike and the Mechanics, George Clinton, Morrissey, Squeeze, Skunk Anansie, Erasure and Billy Bragg among the acts to play here. Suede played a fan-club only gig as part of the filming of the video for their 'Filmstar' single.

The Island had a good reputation among gig-goers and clubbers alike but there was shock in 1996 after three members of security were shot in the foyer, one of them fatally wounded, after two men were refused entry to the club after 3am. The Island closed in 2001 and ever since the main part of the building has been in use a banqueting hall currently called The Coliseum Suite. The former club's foyer was used as a pub for a few years but has since become an Indian restaurant.

King's Head

28 Market Place, Romford, RM1 3ER

The King's Head pub on this site dates back to 1678, having been rebuilt in 1898.

The King's Hall at the back of the pub hosted the King's Head Blues Club on Monday nights from 1969 putting on respected up-and-coming acts from the blues circuit. This was a sister venue to The Village Blues Club held every Saturday at the Roundhouse in Dagenham. Bands on their way to success to play here included Fleetwood Mac, Black Sabbath, Uriah Heep, Van der Graaf Generator, Traffic, Edgar Broughton, Deep Purple, Pink Fairies, Savoy Brown, The Liverpool Scene and Ten Years After. There were a couple of all-night gigs held on Fridays in 1970. The club also hosted some older established artists such as Zoot Money, Jimmy McGriff, Freddie King and Howlin' Wolf. A young Lee Collinson (later Brilleaux) travelled after school to Romford to see Howlin' Wolf. He later told Radio 2 that the gig had a profound effect on him and was

a big influence on him when fronting Dr Feelgood.

The gigs at The King's Head finished in 1971 as the pub closed down. It was later demolished and replaced by retail.

Incidentally the Roundhouse in Dagenham is not included in this book as it still hosts live music!

Leyton Baths

825 High Road, Leyton, E10 7AA

Leyton Baths were Art Deco style swimming baths built in 1934. The main pool was drained and covered over for the winter months, and the hall was used for concerts making it one of the largest dance hall venues in East London.

LEYTON SUPER BATHS, - LEYTON, E.10

MONDAY 8th APRIL, 1963

The Fabulous

Beatles

Bus Routes, 35, 38, 38a, 69, 249, 257, 234, 70, 170, 26 .
NEAREST UNDERGROUND: LEYTON (CENTRAL)

During the 1950s there were dances with live music from big bands with bandleaders such as Ronnie Scott, Eric Delaney and John Dankworth. During the 1960s among the acts to have played the Baths were The Beatles, The Rolling Stones, Screaming Lord Sutch, The Yardbirds, The Troggs, Small Faces, Tom Jones, Joe Brown, Johnny Kidd and the Pirates and Status Quo. The Kinks played here on the day that their Kinda Kinks album was released in 1965. There was frequent tension at the concerts caused by a mixture of mods and bikers attending these gigs and violence often broke out between these rival groups outside the venue. Some people have suggested that the fighting is what put an end to the concerts here.

LEYTON BATHS   HIGH ROAD
LEYTON, E.10

SMALL FACES

SAT
28
OCT
7.30 to 11.30
7/6

EVERY SATURDAY   POP DANCING

Buy your tickets now! Send to KENNETH JOHNSON LTD.
193 Earlham Grove, London, E.7.   MAR 7032/7089

Please forward............tickets (7/6 each) to

(Name and address) for the SMALL FACES Dance. I enclose

cheque, P/O for............and stamped addressed env.

BUSES: 69, 38, 38A, 170, 249, 257, 6B, 34, 35, 35B

The hall was also used for roller skating, wrestling and the notorious gangsters the Kray Twins were among many who used to compete in boxing matches held here.

Leyton Baths closed in 1991 and was demolished soon afterwards. It was replaced by a Tesco supermarket.

Leyton Baths

London Arena

36 Limeharbour, Isle of Dogs, E14 9TH

The London Arena (aka London Docklands Arena) opened in 1989 in a converted warehouse once used by Fred Olsen Ltd for storing fruit from the Canary Islands, unloaded from their ships berthed on the adjacent Millwall Dock.

The venue had a seating capacity of 15,000. Events ranged from sport events like basketball, ice hockey, wrestling, darts and boxing to music concerts and trade exhibitions. Duran Duran were the first band to headline the Arena. Other headliners included Britney Spears, Pink Floyd, David Bowie, Eminem, Simply Red, Westlife, Rod Stewart, Muse, Justin Timberlake, Red Hot Chili Peppers, Guns 'n' Roses, Destiny's Child, Bob Dylan, Eurythmics and New Kids On The Block. Concerts by Erasure, Slipknot, S Club 7 and Will Young were recorded and released on video. Scenes from the Robbie Williams video for 'She's the One' were filmed inside the arena.

The 1998 and 1999 Brit Awards were held at the arena, and from 1989 until 2001 it was also the venue for the Smash Hits Poll Winners Party. The event was notorious for a commotion live on TV in 1991 involving presenter Phillip Schofield and Carter USM, when the band's performance was cut short, causing them to trash the stage. When Schofield made a remark about the band's behaviour, their guitarist Fruitbat rugby-tackled Schofield to the ground.

London Arena struggled to make a profit and closed in 2005. Between closure and demolition,

it housed the annual 'Crisis Open Christmas' event where homeless people were provided with food and accommodation.

The building was demolished in 2006 and has since been replaced by a residential development. The Crossharbour and London Arena DLR station was renamed to simply Crossharbour. However, the London Arena name still remains on a few street signs in the area.

Lotus Ballroom Club

22-26 Woodgrange Road, Forest Gate, E7 0QH

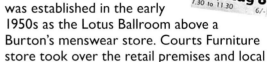

This venue was established in the early 1950s as the Lotus Ballroom above a Burton's menswear store. Courts Furniture store took over the retail premises and local boxer and promoter Kenny Johnson took over the lease to the Ballroom in 1962. Due to his contacts he attracted influential bands to the venue, many of them playing on their Kavern Club nights. The bands included Graham Bond Organisation, John Mayall and The Bluesbreakers, Nashville Teens, Johnny Lonesome and the Travellers, The Kinks and The Merseybeats. The BBC filmed a Screaming Lord Sutch and the Savages gig in 1964 for a documentary about Sutch who had gained notoriety with his horror-themed stage shows as well as for standing as a parliamentary candidate.

The Ballroom was renamed the Lotus Club by the middle of the decade and

continued to put on successful nights attracting customers such as West Ham footballers Bobby Moore and Geoff Hurst. Bands that played around that period included The Attack, Small Faces, The Move, The Electric Prunes, The Foundations and The Moody Blues. The club also put on US acts such as The Temptations, Little Eva, Martha Reeves & the Vandellas. Mary Wells' performance in 1967 in front of 600 people attracted the club's biggest ever turnout.

By the late 1960s the club's emphasis on live music declined in favour of pre-recorded music and usage as a casino and restaurant. It eventually closed in 2002 and the floors above the shop (now Poundland) have been converted into flats.

New All-Star Club

9a Artillery Passage, Spitalfields, E1 7LJ

This small club situated in an alleyway close to Liverpool Street Station operated from 1965 to 1968 and hosted live acts from Fridays to Sundays.

The Equals and The Rick 'n' Beckers played residencies at the club. Many American touring acts also played, including Edwin Starr, Screaming Jay Hawkins, Ben E. King, Pattie LaBelle, Wilson Pickett, The Amboy Dukes, Stevie Wonder and Sugar Pie Desanto. Home-grown talent to play here included Zoot Money, David Essex and The Mood Indigo, Bluesology (who included Reg Dwight, the future Elton John) and The Shevells.

In a 1967 edition of Melody Maker the club advertised a 'mini skirt, dancing and hair fashion competition' on Monday and Thursday evenings.

The early 18th century property has been Grade II listed since 1973 and these days it is a private residence.

Ocean

270 Mare Street, Hackney, E8 1HE

Ocean opened up as Hackney's flagship community arts centre in 2001 in a 1920s building formerly known as the Methodist Central Hall and also incorporated the adjacent former Central Library.

Ocean had a capacity for 2,100 people and cost £23 million of public money but was run as an independent venue. It had three different venue spaces of various sizes with six bars. The events covered all musical genres and hosted live music and a range of club-nights often for big multi-room UK garage, hip-hop and R&B events.

The venue opened with two nights by Soft Cell (their first gigs for 17 years) followed by a four-night residency by the Fun Lovin' Criminals. Broadcast on TV was the MTV 5 Night Stand event which included headliners The Stereophonics, Papa Roach, Toploader, Damage and Five. Subsequent MTV 5 Night Stands here over the following years included performances by Super Furry Animals, James Brown, Garbage, The Orb, Daryl Hall and John Oates, Gary Numan, Dionne Warwick, David Byrne, Belinda Carlisle, Sparks and Level 42. Other acts to perform at Ocean included The Damned, Patti Smith, Ladytron, The Wonderstuff, Therapy? and Squarepusher. On the 10th anniversary of the death of Freddie Mercury the Queen fan club held a special party at Ocean with SAS Band headlining who were joined by Queen's Brian May and Roger Taylor for a few songs. A Stiff Little Fingers performance was recorded and released as the Still Kicking CD and DVD.

Ocean gained a poor reputation after several violent incidents, including up to 150 youths pelting police with bricks and bottles after an under-18s La Cosa Nostra Grime rave in 2004. The profits accumulated running as a music venue were planned to fund other arts projects though failure to break even led it to entering into administration and Ocean closed down in 2004.

In 2011, the building reopened as an independent cinema called the Hackney Picturehouse.

Odeon Ilford

Eastern Avenue, Gants Hill, Ilford, IG2 6DD

ODEON THEATR
GANTS HILL ILFORD 554 2

OUTLAW ARTISTS presen
**THE TOM
ROBINSON BAN**
at 7.30 p.m.
MONDAY
APRIL
9
STALLS £2.50

NO TICKET EXCHANGED
NOR MONEY REFUNDED
This portion to be retained

Located opposite Gants Hill Underground Station this venue with 2,190 seats opened as the Savoy Cinema in 1934 and was renamed the Odeon in 1949. By the late 1950s the Jewish community in the local borough was the largest across Europe, and the Odeon would be filled to capacity when it was used as their main synagogue (while still operating as a cinema) until 1981.

The Odeon was used for gigs between 1977 and 1980 with the old organ pit in front of the stage boarded over and carpeted to enable the crowd to get closer to the stage. Cliff Richard performed here as part of his Tear Fund Gospel Concerts and there were subsequent gigs by the Tom Robinson Band, Dr. Feelgood, Wishbone Ash, Graham Parker and The Rumour and Hawkwind. Ian Dury and The Blockheads played here four times over 1978 and 1979, with the December 1978 concert recorded and released as the Straight from the Desk live album. During an instrumental break in 'Clever Trevor' Dury name checks West Ham United F.C., Gants Hill and Ilford much to the delight of the local fans. The crowd was so lively that the boarded over organ pit gave way under the crowd pressure causing Dury to warn the audience to mind the hole in

his introduction to 'Hit Me with Your Rhythm Stick'. He would mention it repeatedly later in the set. A less spectacular event was when only 100 people showed up to see Jean Jacques Burnel's Euroman Cometh album tour, although the small crowd did get to witness an onstage punch up between Burnel and his guitarist.

By the time the cinema closed in 2002 it had five screens. Following a couple of illegal rave parties, the building was demolished in 2003 and a block of flats now occupies the site.

Odeon Romford

108 South Street, Romford, RM1 1SS

Originally opened in 1936 as the Havana Cinema with a seating capacity of 2,500. It was renamed the Odeon in 1949.

The Odeon put on several package tours from the late 1950s into the 1960s where Cliff Richard and The Shadows, Billy Fury, The Rolling Stones, The Honeycombs, Lulu and The Luvvers, The Animals, Johnny Kidd and The Pirates, Gene Vincent and The Beatles all performed. The Bee Gees played in 1968 and the early 1970s saw concerts by Barclay James Harvest, Deep Purple, Four Tops, Detroit Spinners and David Bowie. The latter was on his Ziggy Stardust tour whereby the Romford Recorder newspaper reported that it was "a miracle no one was killed" in the frenzied teenage hysteria both inside and outside the venue. A policeman was injured in the melee as Bowie's car drove away after the gig.

The Odeon was divided up into a multi-screen cinema in 1974 which put an end to live events. It closed in 1990 and the building is currently occupied by ATIK nightclub.

Plastic People

147-149 Curtain Road, Shoreditch, EC2A 3QE

Plastic People originally started off in the West End at 37 Oxford Street in 1995 before moving to this Shoreditch basement location in 2000.

The Shoreditch club had a capacity for around 200 people and had a reputation for its low lighting and heavy sound system. A club night called FWD>> was influential in the UK dubstep scene and became the hub for a new style that became known as dubstep. The club also hosted other popular nights including CDR and Co-Op which were mainly DJ-based but over its life various live acts also performed at Plastic People including The Unicorns, The Long Blondes, Battant, Alexander Robotnick, Thomas Fehlmann, Animal Collective, The Field and Inga Copeland.

In 2015 the club closed down after the owners simply decided to call it a day.

The premises are now occupied by The Sunset Bar.

Pleasure Unit

359 Bethnal Green Road, Bethnal Green, E2 6LG

This Victorian pub was originally called the White Hart and then various names before it was renamed the Pleasure Unit in 2001.

The Pleasure Unit was, for a few years, a regular venue for (mainly) up-and-coming bands. The venue was often criticised for having no draught beer and a poor-quality sound system. Nevertheless, it was a popular place to play. Acts included The Cuban Heels, Redjetson, Bow Mods, The Long Blondes, The Charlie Parkers, Luxembourg, The Buff Medways, Rhesus, Fades, Ciccone, Neils Children, Cats and Cats and Cats, Metro Riots and Pete Doherty

The pub was renamed the Star of Bethnal Green in 2008 and functions as a successful bar/club with DJs but rarely has any live music.

Wed 7 Sep '05
The Pleasure Unit
359 Bethnal Green Rd
London E.2
Bethnal Green
(Central Line)
On stage 9.00
Entrance £5

Rex

361-375 High Street, Stratford, E15 4QZ

The Rex originally opened as the Borough Theatre and Opera House in 1896 and the venue was known as the "Drury Lane of the East" owing to the lavish interior which attracted top name stars and productions. After a refit it reopened in 1933 as the Rex Cinema and eventually became a bingo hall in 1969, where Manfred Mann's Earth Band played in 1972 in what seemed to be a one-off gig for the venue which reverted to a cinema in 1974 for a brief spell before laying derelict for over 20 years.

The Rex was restored and became a concert venue and club in 1997 and saw gigs by The Prodigy, Fugazi, Foo Fighters, Dizzee Rascal, Buju Banton, Usher, Jah Shaka, Bone Thugs-n-Harmony and Foxy Brown. A 2008 show by Lil Wayne was cut short after missiles were thrown from the crowd and fights broke out in the overcrowded VIP area at the side of the stage. The Guardian reported that Lil Wayne was dragged off stage by a security guard apparently due to threats on his life. In 1999 a doorman at the Rex was shot dead as gig-goers arrived for a show by Beenie Man. Two people were also injured by ricochets.

The club was repossessed by the council in 2010 and after a refurbishment it re-opened in 2012 as Sync which presented DJs, stand-up comedy, boxing matches and a private VIP section boasting views over Stratford High Street. Sync closed down after a short time and the former cinema reopened again in 2017 but this time as an indoor trampoline park called ZAPspace.

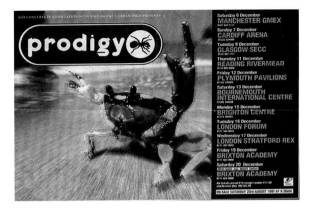

The Rezz

27 North Street, Romford, RM1 1BA

The Rezz was a club held in the basement under a row of shops.

The club held popular jazz, funk and soul nights at weekends during the 1980s. The Rezz hosted an Indie/Alternative night every Wednesday where live bands also played between 1983 and 1988. Bands to play here included The Triffids, The Shamen, Screaming Blue Messiahs, The Bolshoi, Felt, My Bloody Valentine, Nitzer Ebb, The Prisoners, The Revillos and local band The Wolfhounds. Underworld who were also based in Romford, deny that their single 'Rez' was anything to do with this club.

The premises continued as a nightclub after being renamed Charmers then The Cellar Bar but closed around 2008 and was subsequently bulldozed along with the neighbouring shops. Building work started on a new block in 2010 though promptly came to a halt leaving an uncompleted concrete structure ever since.

Room at the Top

197 High Street, Ilford, IG1 1IX

Opening in 1961, Room at the Top was located in the penthouse of the newly rebuilt Harrison Gibson furniture store after the previous building had been destroyed by fire. The venue had a direct independent lift access from the High Street.

It initially opened as a 250-seat cabaret venue with Petula Clark performing on the opening night,

followed by popular entertainers such as Mel Tormé, Matt Monro, Roy Castle, Anita Harris, and Danny La Rue plus a two-week residency by teen idol Adam Faith. From 1965 the venue dropped the live entertainment and concentrated on its casino and restaurant business though there was a brief return to cabaret a few years later before it became a discotheque with the Room at the Top calling itself "Ilford's Disco in the Sky". It hosted popular events such as a Wednesday Night Fever dance competition. In 1974 Elton John celebrated his 27th birthday here and performed some songs.

During the 1980s it hosted a multitude of different live acts including Chas 'n' Dave, Marmalade, Shakatak, My Bloody Valentine, Breathless, The Chesterfields, Talulah Gosh and The Dallas Boys. Live music stopped but the venue carried on as a nightclub until 2010, albeit with diminishing attendances during the latter years.

The building is currently being refurbished and converted mainly into flats.

The Spitz

109 Commercial Street, Spitalfields, E1 6BG

The Spitz was a popular bar, gallery and cafe with live music most nights in a 250-capacity room upstairs featuring jazz, folk, blues and rock among its genres. It opened here in Old Spitalfields Market in 1996 with performances by Julie Felix and Bert Jansch on the opening night. Many acts performed there over the next decade including Billy Bragg, The Men They Couldn't Hang, Joan As Police Woman, Richard Hawley, Low, Billy Childish, Athlete, Adele, Kate Nash, The Newtown Neurotics, The Blue Aeroplanes, The Bluetones, Seasick Steve, John Parish, John Renbourn, Keane and The Libertines,

Regeneration of the adjacent market resulted in the developers serving notice to The Spitz to quit the premises. The last show took place in 2007 and featured many of the musicians who had played there regularly over the years, such as Terry Edwards & The Scapegoats, Seb Rochford, Sandy Dillon and Beth Orton. The event was filmed and later reappeared as the documentary A Great Night in the Spitz.

These days the premises are home to a fashion retailer called '& Other Stories'. The Spitz name lives on as the former managing director of the venue founded the Spitz Charitable Trust taking musicians to people who do not have regular access to live music in places such as residential care homes and day centres.

Sundown

401 Mile End Road, Mile End, E3 4PB

Situated opposite Mile End Underground station, this was previously the Art Deco style Odeon Theatre, one of a few cinemas converted into a small chain of live venues and discos called Sundown Clubs (see also Edmonton and Charing Cross Road).

The Sundown in Mile End opened in 1972 with Slade breaking away from their USA tour especially for the opening concert before immediately flying back to resume the tour. The 2,500 capacity venue was a sell out that night and Melody Maker reported "It was a revival of 'Beatlemania' atmosphere that this hall and band had generated". Bands to subsequently play the venue included Electric Light Orchestra with support from the Velvet Underground, Fleetwood Mac, Stray, Amon Düül II, Status Quo, Home, Genesis, Wizzard, Crowbar, The J. Geils Band, Byzantium, Fanny and New York Dolls. The venue continued to run films on non music days, using the circle seating.

This Mile End venue as a Sundown Club had a short life and closed the following year in 1973 after the owners said that they were going to concentrate on the Edmonton Sundown for major concerts. After laying empty it became the Liberty Cinema in 1975 screening Asian films before finally closing in 1978.

SUNDOWN MILE END E3

WEDNESDAY 22nd NOVEMBER
CROWBAR
GNIDROLOG

THURSDAY 23rd NOVEMBER
FLEETWOOD MAC
McKENDREE SPRING

WEDNESDAY 29th NOVEMBER
ALAN BOWN
CAROL GRIMES AND UNCLE DOG

THURSDAY 30th NOVEMBER
E.L.O.
VELVET UNDERGROUND

SUNDOWN EDMONTON N18

THURSDAY 23rd NOVEMBER
CROWBAR
GNIDROLOG

FRIDAY 24th NOVEMBER
INCREDIBLE STRING BAND

FRIDAY 1st DECEMBER
ARGENT
McKENDREE SPRING

FRIDAY 29th DECEMBER
HAWKWIND
THE SPACE RITUAL

SUNDOWN BRIXTON SW9

THURSDAY 30th NOVEMBER
THE HARVESTMOBILE TOUR

FRIDAY 1st DECEMBER
MICK GREENWOOD BAND
GNIDROLOG

SUNDAY 10th DECEMBER
OSIBISA
SILVERHEAD

SATURDAY 30th DECEMBER
HAWKWIND
THE SPACE RITUAL

The building was demolished in 1984 and an office block was built on the site although that currently stands vacant.

NORTH

The Bell

257-259 Pentonville Road, Kings Cross, N1 9NL

The Bell, built in the 1830s, was notorious during the 1930s as a base for Big Alf White, one of London's most violent gangsters during the interwar period. In the 1970s a few punk bands such as The Damned, The Killjoys and Neo played at the pub but a Subway Sect gig in 1977 was memorable for all the wrong reasons when Henry Bowles, a friend of The Clash died after his head was pushed through a window by the pub's bouncers. Bowles was name checked in the lyrics of 'London Bouncers' by Action Pact and there's also a dedication in the sleeve notes of The Clash's London Calling.

The pub was a well-loved gay haunt during the 1980s and also hosted a mix of bands including Phil Lynott's Grand Slam, Faithful Breath, Amazulu, Serious Drinking, The X-Men, Erasure and the first ever gig by Bronski Beat who, at the time, only knew six songs but were so enthusiastically received by the audience they played them all again as an encore. The pub held fundraising events including the Lesbians Benefit for the Miners when Tapanda Re and The Gymslips played.

The Bell has seen many name changes over the years including spells as Crossbar and Sahara Nights. It's currently called the Big Chill, a bar serving food and hosting DJs at the weekends.

Coliseum

25-26 Manor Park Road, Harlesden, NW10 4JJ

The Coliseum was a cinema that originally opened as the Picture Theatre in 1912 with seating for 850 customers.

The venue did not feature regular gigs, it mainly screened Bollywood and unlicensed kung fu movies, though it did host a notable punk bill in 1977. The Clash headlined with support from Buzzcocks, Subway Sect and the debut live appearance by The Slits. This was also the first Buzzcocks gig without Howard Devoto. An unofficial live album of the Clash gig, called Harlesden's Burning, has been released in recent years.

By the 1980s the cinema screened adult films and also hosted reggae nights with DJs and live acts including Jah Shaka, Little John, Eli Immanuel and Prince Hammer. The Coliseum closed in the mid 1980s and was derelict for a few years before being restored as a JD Wetherspoon pub called The Coliseum. That closed and reopened as The Misty Moon which held regular live tribute bands and Irish music. The pub then changed ownership in 2015 and was renamed Harlesden Picture Palace though this closed down in 2017. Prior to closing the pub hosted the Harlesden is Still Burning gig, with The Electrics headlining, for the anniversary of the punk gig 40 years earlier.

The building remains boarded up at the time of writing.

The Cross Kings

126 York Way, N1 0AX

This pub was originally The City of York Tavern. Later it was renamed The Backpacker for a few years and then The Cross Kings in 2006.

The Cross Kings was a quirky Bohemian venue and was well-loved for live music and comedy acts with mixed events often on the same night operating over two floors. Bands that played here include The Men That Will Not Be Blamed for Nothing, The Dead Roads, Kill Cartel, Skat Injector, Filthy Pedro, Slashed Seat Affair, The Molotovs, MJ Hibbett and The Validators, She Makes War, Katharine Blake, Alright the Captain, Four Tet, Television Personalities and The Gaa Gaas. There were also DJ club nights, open mic sessions and film screenings.

The Cross Kings closed in 2010 and reopened as The Star of Kings amid much regeneration in the vicinity of the pub.

CLUB HELL
FRIDAY 26H JUNE
8-2am

F*CK
GLASTONBURY

£6
£4
with
flyer

HEAT FROM A DEAD STAR
THE SUICIDAL BIRDS
PONY PACK
MARCIA MELLO

THE CROSS KINGS
126 YORK WAY, KINGS CROSS, N1 0AX

DEAD AND BURIED
DEATHROCK, TRAD GOTH, POST PUNK
GOTHABILLY + GRAVEYARD GARAGE
80's NDW, HORROR PUNK, NEW WAVE
OLD SCHOOL PUNK....

WITH DJ CAVEY NIK + GUESTS

SATURDAY 26TH JANUARY
SATURDAY 23RD FEBRUARY
SATURDAY 29TH MARCH
SATURDAY 26TH APRIL
SATURDAY 31ST MAY
SATURDAY 28TH JUNE

THE CROSS KINGS
[JESTER BAR]
126 YORK WAY
KINGS CROSS
N1 0AX

0207 278 83 18

www.thecrosskings.co.uk
[MODEL: MISS JAIDIAN]

21.00 - 02.00
R.O.A.R

DEAD AND BURIED 26 07 08

RATS OVER LONDON

Kamo

CAVEY NIK
DEAD & BURIED HOSTS RATS OVER MILAN
THE CROSS KINGS
YORK WAY
N1 0AX
21.00 - 02.00

M DECAY

---

xxTRYHARDER PROMOTIONSxx
presents

THE SETUP
FORFEIT
GET FUCKING DEAD
COLD SNAP
VICE CITY!
SATURDAY JULY 4TH
DOORS AT 7 6 QUID ADV 8 QUID OTD
THE CROSS KINGS LONDON
FOR TICKETS CONTACT www.myspace.com/xxtryharderxx

8pm-
midnight

The Trashville Lounge
Presents
ZEN MOTEL
RUBELLA
Trail of Disgrace
Erin K
+ 5o's go-go movies
+ DJ Grae j
Thurs. March 12
The Cross Kings
126 York Way, London, N1 0AX
0207 278 8318

£6/£5 with flyer

Lo-fi, diy, trash, country, blues 'n' punk!
myspace.com/trashvilleworld   trashville.co.uk

21.00 - 02.00
R.O.A.R

Country Club

210a Haverstock Hill, Belsize Park, NW3 2AG

Situated in a tennis club up an alleyway near Belsize Park station this venue put on occasional gigs from the early 1960s including one by The Rolling Stones in 1964.

Between 1968 and 1971 the Club became a regular gig venue. Hawkwind played here seven times during their early years and Muddy Waters and his Blues Band played a six-night residency in 1970. What would have been The Graham Bond Initiation's debut gig was cancelled at the last minute after Bond was arrested during the soundcheck on a bankruptcy charge. He was taken to Pentonville Prison until ex band member Jack Bruce bailed him out. Other acts to have played at this venue include Pink Floyd, The Pretty Things, Jimi Hendrix Experience, Spooky Tooth, Sly and the Family Stone, David Bowie, Soft Machine, Yes and Ten Years After. Elton John is said to have appeared onstage in 1970 in tennis gear straight from the court.

Drummer Ginger Johnson then took over the club renaming it the Iroko Country Club which hosted live music from the likes of Cymande and popular African musicians including Fela Kuti, Osibisa and Assagai. Thin Lizzy used to rehearse here in 1974 and participated in many of the venue's jam sessions. Later in the 1970s, following the death of Johnson, the Iroko was closed and demolished. The Aspern Grove housing development now stands on the site.

Dominion/ABC Harrow

79 Station Road, Harrow, HA1 2TU

The 2,000 capacity Dominion Cinema opening night in 1936 consisted of films, Joseph Muscant and his orchestra and live variety acts.

Various live acts played here over the years including a concert by 17-year-old teen idol Paul Anka in 1958. In 1962 the cinema was re-named the ABC and the Art Deco façade was covered over in metal cladding for the rest of its life as a cinema.

The ABC hosted a few pop music concerts during the 1960s. These included shows by Cliff Richard and The Shadows, The Animals and Jerry Lee Lewis early in 1964 and later that year there was a package tour of The Kinks, Gerry and the Pacemakers, Gene Pitney and Marianne Faithfull all playing two shows on the one evening. The 1965 package tour saw a two-show bill of Brian Poole and The Tremeloes, Dave Berry and The Cruisers, Billy Fury and The Gamblers and The Pretty Things. The Harrow Light Opera Company also ran a program of events at the venue all through the 1960s

In 1972 the ABC was divided into two and a smaller cinema was made of the former circle with the former stalls area becoming a bingo club and later a church. The name changed to the Canon Cinema and finally the Safari until it was closed in 2020 due to the Covid-19 pandemic.

The main part of the building will be demolished as part of redevelopment into flats. Preparation work began in 2021 with the removal of the metal cladding revealing the facade which will be retained and restored as part of the redevelopment.

Duke of Lancaster

6 Lancaster Road, New Barnet, EN4 8AS

The Duke of Lancaster was a Victorian pub that became popular with the pub rock music scene in the 1970s. Toyah played here twice in 1978 who incidentally released an album the following year called Sheep Farming in Barnet. Iron Maiden played a gig here in 1979 and new wave bands The Vapors, The Accidents and Dead Fingers Talk played here around that period as did many popular local and small touring rock bands, including A Touch of Class, Bleak House and the Fabulous Feedback Band, right up to the pub's demise in 2002.

One of the most famous band associations is that The Stranglers used to play here in 1975 before they were famous. To get around their Greater London Council ban from London venues and after building up a loyal fan following and enjoying chart success the band played here in 1978 as one of a trio of secret pub gigs to thank those venues and their landlords for their support during the band's rise to success. The gig took place on Valentine's Day and the band were joined onstage by Laura Logic of X Ray Spex on saxophone. It was so crammed that condensation was dripping from the ceiling and had crowds of fans outside who were unable to squeeze into the pub.

The pub was demolished in 2002 and a block of flats has since been built on the site.

DUKE OF LANCASTER
Approach Road, NEW BARNET
(beside BR New Barnet)

Thursday July 5th
BACKLASH
Friday July 6th
JOHN GRIMALDI'S CHEAP FLIGHTS
Saturday July 7th
DOG WATCH
Sunday July 8th
RAM
Tuesday July 10th
MEDIA

DUKE OF LANCASTER
Approach Road, NEW BARNET
(beside BR New Barnet)

Thursday July 26th
THE VAPORS
Friday July 27th
CLIENTELE
Saturday July 28th
TOTAL STRANGERS
Sunday July 29th
WILD LIFE
Tuesday July 31st
COLD SHOULDER BAND

—MELODY MAKER, May 19, 1979
Saturday
DUKE OF LANCASTER
New Barnet
64 SPOONS
Our final gig at
the Duke, be early
IRON MAIDEN
BANDWAGON, KINGSBURY CIRCLE

Tuesday
DUKE OF LANCASTER
Lancaster Road, New Barnet
THE RATS
WE ARE THE NEW WAVE

The Enterprise

2 Haverstock Hill, Chalk Farm, London NW3 2BL

The small upstairs room of The Enterprise held popular folk nights during the 1960s where Paul Simon once played along with others on the folk circuit such as Joe Stead, Shirley Collins, Strawbs and Sandy Denny. There was also a resident band called The Folk Enterprise.

Dan Treacy of Television Personalities ran The Room At The Top club here during 1985 and 1986 where his own band often played alongside other indie bands of the time such as That Petrol Emotion, Go! Service, The Housemartins, Shop Assistants, The Pastels, The June Brides, The Mighty Lemon Drops, The Membranes and The Wedding Present.

During the 2000s the venue hosted up-and-coming acts The Darkness, The Crimea, James Blunt and Eliza Doolittle as well as many established artists such as Ian Broudie, Viv Albertine and Jon Fratelli. Gemma Hayes played four sold out nights in 2006. In 2014 and 2015 the venue was one used for the Camden Rocks annual mini festival which operated at multiple venues simultaneously with one wristband enabling audience admission to all the venues. Kenelis, Mia Klose, WACO, Strangefruit, and The Assist were some acts to play here as part of that festival over the two years.

Gigs at The Enterprise sadly ceased in 2015 and these days the pub's upper floors serve as a boutique hotel.

The Enterprise

Finsbury Park Empire

2 St Thomas's Road, N4 2QG

The Finsbury Park Empire opened in 1910 and was one of many variety theatres in the Moss Empires Theatres UK chain. The company regarded this 2,000-seat venue second in line to Moss Empires number one theatre, the London Palladium.

Well-known music hall and variety entertainers of their time appeared at the Empire with stars such as Lily Langtree, Houdini and Marie Lloyd performing there in the early years through to Laurel and Hardy, Tony Hancock and Tommy Cooper during the 1950s. The 1950s also saw shows by early rock and roll and skiffle acts with Tommy Steele playing six nights in a row in 1956 and for another six nights with The Vipers in 1957. Country singer Mitchell Torok played a 12-night residency in 1957 and Shirley Bassey performed for seven nights in 1958. Adam Faith with support act The John Barry Seven had a run of six nights in 1960 as did Duane Eddy. Also in 1960 a double bill of Eddie Cochrane and Gene Vincent with support from Georgie Fame ran for six nights, just a week before Cochrane's fatal car crash in Wiltshire.

Max Miller proclaimed that variety was all over as he left the Empire's stage in 1959 after performing in front of an audience of only thirty people. Due to the decline in popularity of variety performances and the coming of television the Empire closed to the public in 1960 with the final headliners being Emile Ford and the Checkmates. Also on the bill were The Lana Sisters, featuring the future Dusty Springfield. The Empire was used a year after closing for filming scenes for the The Young Ones starring Cliff Richard who had previously played the venue over a dozen times.

The building was demolished in 1965 and a block of flats called Vaudeville Court now occupies the site. A plaque on the current building remembers the history of the site. Chas McDevitt, who also performed on the very last bill in 1960, was present at the unveiling.

The Galtymore

194 Cricklewood Broadway, Cricklewood, NW2 3EB

The Galtymore opened in 1952 as a massive dancing and entertainment venue and was regarded as the place to go for Irish emigrants who had made their way to London. This part of North West London had a particularly large population of Irish people.

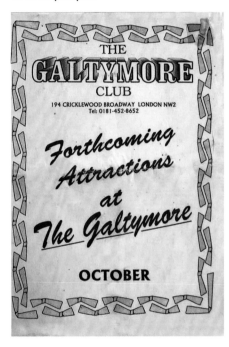

THE
GALTYMORE
CLUB
194 CRICKLEWOOD BROADWAY LONDON NW2
Tel: 0181-452-8652

Forthcoming Attractions at The Galtymore

OCTOBER

The venue was a popular place with two huge dance-halls to hear music from the Irish country and showband scene. Over the years popular acts to appear include The Wolfe Tones, Joe Dolan, Brian Coll, Declan Nearney, The Westernaires and Philomena Begley. The record attendance was for a performance in 1967 by Larry Cunningham and The Mighty Avons, who in Ireland had recently knocked the Beatles off the number one singles chart slot. The Irish Post reported that a total of 6,850 paying customers attended that night in the Galtymore. A rare event away from the usual Irish music was when The Fall supported by John Cooper Clarke played two nights in 2006.

The Galtymore closed in 2008 with regular performer Big Tom and The Mainliners playing the final night to a packed-out venue. A previous concert of theirs at the club in 2004 was released as a live DVD.

The building has now been demolished with plans to build a supermarket and flats on the (currently) vacant site. The venue is remembered in Brendan Shine's song 'Where did you Meet Her? (I Met Her in the Galtymore)'.

Gaumont State Cinema
197-199 Kilburn High Rd, NW6 7HY

When the Gaumont State opened in 1937 it was one of the biggest cinemas in Europe with seating for over 4,000 people. The building was the work of architect George Coles (see also the Trocadero in Elephant and Castle and the Odeon in Woolwich) its design being inspired by the Empire State Building in New York City.

Entertainers including Gracie Fields and George Formby performed at the official opening of the cinema which was broadcast live on BBC Radio. Fields and Formby returned the following year to share the bill with Paul Robeson and Max Miller in a show to raise funds for refugee children from Nazi Germany. Another refugee benefit show was held in 1939 when Sidney Torch played a special programme of music which the Nazis had banned in Germany. Django Reinhardt, Stéphane Grappelli, Dinah Shore, Frank Sinatra, Louis Armstrong, Count Basie Orchestra, Harry Belafonte, Tubby Hayes, Ted Heath, Johnny Dankworth and Humphrey Lyttelton all performed here. The onset of rock and roll brought Buddy Holly and the Crickets, Bill Haley and His Comets, Cliff Richard and The Shadows and Jerry Lee Lewis to the State in the late 1950s. In the 1960s Ella Fitzgerald, The Beatles, The Animals, Dizzy Gillespie, Art Blakey and The Rolling Stones all played here and rock acts into the 1970s included Jethro Tull, Faces, Black Sabbath and Alvin Lee. The BBC broadcast a Deep Purple concert from the State in 1974 which was later released as the

Live in London album. A 1974 Ronnie Wood concert billed as Woody and Friends was later released as an album and DVD The First Barbarians: Live from Kilburn. The band included Keith Richards, Ian McLagan and Rod Stewart. A 1977 concert by The Who was recorded, and small parts used for the documentary film The Kids Are Alright and the whole concert was later released on DVD. It was at that concert that the band played Who Are You for the first time. Part of the 1981 video for Ultravox's 'Vienna' was filmed inside the State.

The main auditorium closed as a cinema in 1980 and was used for bingo until 2007. The building re-opened as the Ruach City Church in 2010.

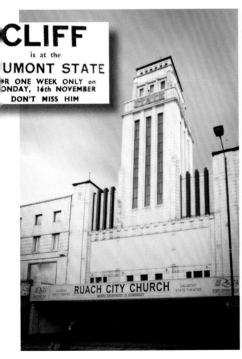

Golders Green Hippodrome

North End Road, Golders Green, NW11 7RP

The Golders Green Hippodrome opened in 1913 as a 2,000 seat music hall, hosting variety shows, pantomimes and performances by the British National Opera Company and the D'Oyly Carte Opera Company. A projection box was also fitted during the 1920s so that films could be shown on Sundays. Musical stars to appear here over the years included Stéphane Grappelli, Django Reinhardt, Chico Marx, Marlene Dietrich and the venue also hosted a rock and roll tour featuring Gene Vincent and Jerry Lee Lewis where the audience danced in the aisles and jumped on the stage leading to an early curtailment of the show.

A final live performance for the venue as a live theatre was in 1968, and featured an eclectic bill including Simon Dupree and the Big Sound, Vera Lynn, Danny la Rue and Status Quo. In 1969 the BBC took over the lease and converted it into a television studio and in 1973 it became a radio concert hall with a reduced capacity of 700 seats. The Hippodrome was home for the BBC Concert Orchestra, and it also saw broadcasts and concerts from the BBC Big Band and BBC Radio Orchestra. Many rock bands played here such as Queen, AC/DC, UFO, Barclay James Harvest, Procol Harum, Nazareth, Meat Loaf, The Cult, Stiff Little Fingers, INXS and 3 Colours Red. A private Christmas concert given by The Jam for members of their fan club in December 1981 was subsequently broadcast by the BBC. Many recordings of these performances have subsequently been released on vinyl/CD often as bootlegs. The Hippodrome was also used by the BBC for broadcasting dramas, boxing and comedy including episodes of Monty Python's Flying Circus in 1969.

In 2003 the BBC left and the building was used as an evangelical church.

In 2017 it was bought by a charity who are planning to use it as an Islamic community centre after being refused planning permission for a mosque as they are prevented from affixing a minaret to a listed building.

BBC
Hippodrome
Theatre,
Golders Green
Home of the
BBC Concert Orchestra
1969-2003
BBC HERITAGE TRAIL

Majestic Ballroom

10 Stroud Green Road, Finsbury Park, N4 2DF

This building started off as a horse-drawn tram depot that was later converted into a roller skating rink before becoming the Rink Cinema in 1909.

In 1920 the capacity was enlarged when the building was joined together with the adjacent Cinematograph Theatre on Seven Sisters Road which it backed onto.

The whole building was converted into the Majestic Ballroom in 1959. Eric Galloway and his 12-piece orchestra were the resident dance band. In 1964, the BBC televised a ballroom

dancing event from the Majestic with music provided by Victor Silvester and the Ballroom Orchestra. There was also occasionally rhythm and blues and jazz with Cyril Stapleton, Stéphane Grappelli, Acker Bilk, Migil 5, The Pretty Things and Alexis Korner's Blues Incorporated all playing during the early 1960s. The only pop concert was when 2,000 people packed into the Majestic to watch Brian Epstein's Mersey Beat Showcase package tour in 1963 featuring The Beatles, Gerry and The Pacemakers, The Big Three and Billy J. Kramer With The Dakotas.

In the mid 1960s the Majestic became the Top Rank Bingo Club which continued until 1984.

The Cinematograph Theatre part of the building was demolished in 1999 and replaced with a Lidl Supermarket. The original Rink Cinema building became a snooker club and is now in use as Rowans Tenpin Bowl. The bowling alley was used in the music video for 'Bruise' by Band of Skulls.

Majestic Ballroom

Michael Sobell Sports Centre

Hornsey Road, Islington, N7 7N

Named after a philanthropist who donated money towards its building in 1973, the Michael Sobell Sports Centre was the UK's first purpose-built inner-city sports centre. It held occasional concerts as well as large scale, often televised, sporting events such as gymnastics, basketball and world boxing championships.

Ian Dury and The Blockheads supported by The Selector played for two nights in 1980 and The Jam played for two nights of pro-CND shows in 1981 with various support bands including Bananarama. The poor reaction to those support acts and guest speakers influenced Weller's decision to split the band a year later as he felt his booing fans were too narrow-minded. After one gig there were running battles as many of their mod fans clashed with punks who were coming out of a gig by The Exploited at the nearby Rainbow Theatre where the headline band had been revving up the crowd performing their 'Fuck the Mods' song. Other gigs that decade included Rainbow supported by Lita Ford for two nights in 1983 and New Order in 1985. The Prodigy performed at the Telepathy rave there in 1991.

These days the venue is the renamed Sobell Leisure Centre but no longer hosts concerts.

MCP PRESENTS

The JAM

Plus Special Guests
2nd IMAGE,
Bananarama and The Rimshots
MICHAEL SOBELL Sports Centre
Sunday December 13th 6.30pm
Tickets £4.50 (Inc. VAT)

MCP PRESENTS

The JAM

Plus Special Guests
DEPT. S
Bananarama and The Questions
MICHAEL SOBELL Sports Centre
Saturday December 12th 6.30pm
Tickets £4.50 (Inc. VAT)

National Ballroom

234 Kilburn High Road, Kilburn, NW6 4JR

Built on the site of a mansion called The Grange this building was opened as The Grange Cinema in 1914. With over 2,000 seats this was the biggest cinema in Kilburn until the huge Gaumont State opened in 1937. The Grange cinema closed down in 1975.

The Grange was converted into a nightclub called the National Club and later became known as the National Ballroom. It started off as an Irish club hosting acts such as The Bothy Band who performed here for a BBC Radio One Live In Concert session in 1978. The early 1980s onwards saw more mainstream chart and alternative acts play here including Dexys Midnight Runners, New Order, Feargal Sharkey, Cocteau Twins, The Sisters of Mercy, Jesus and Mary Chain, Happy Mondays, The Pixies and Sonic Youth. The Smith's performance in 1986 was recorded and released as the live album Rank.

During the 1990s James, Blur, The Charlatans, Paul Weller, Beck, Bush, Kula Shaker, Snuff, The Lightning Seeds, Suede, Super Furry Animals and Nirvana all played here. The National was used in the film Backbeat for scenes where the Beatles played at the Star Club in Hamburg. The short-lived 1991 Channel 4 music show Friday at the Dome was broadcast from the National and showed live performances from Lush, Level 42, Robert Palmer and Inspiral Carpets.

The local council refused two attempts by the owners to demolish the building and English Heritage have issued protection by awarding it Grade II listed status.

The National closed in 1999 and the building is currently occupied by the Universal Church of the Kingdom of God.

WED MAY 3rd **PANIC STATION** The 2nd Birthday Party
SOUNDS **KILBURN NATIONAL BALLROOM**
234 KILBURN HIGH ROAD NW6

HAPPYMONDAYS
THE SHAMEN
THE BAND of HOLY JOY
THE JAZZ BUTCHER THE S
STITCH **KING OF THE SLUMS**

JLP CONCERTS PRESENT
special guests
EINSTUERZENDE
Showaddywaddy
MONDAY
7th SEPTEMBER
8pm
Tickets £5.00 in advance
NEUBAUTEN
1st PERFORMANCE FOR 2 YEARS
ONLY PERFORMANCE THIS DECADE
ALL MUSIC PROGRAMMED BY
SOME BIZZARE
NATIONAL CLUB
KILBURN HIGH ROAD LONDON NW6
Tel: 01-328 3141
(+Careys, adjacent to National Club)

METROPOLIS MUSIC PRESENT
JESUS JONES
THE NATIONAL CLUB
234 KILBURN HIGH RD, NW6
THURSDAY 17th MAY
£6.50 Adv. Doors 7.30pm

THE NATIONAL BALLROOM
234 KILBURN HIGH ROAD, NW6
TUESDAY 16 DECEMBER
at 7.30 p.m.
Camouflage presents
JESUS & MARY CHAIN
Nº 855
TO BE RETAINED   NO RE-ADMISSION

SONIC YOUTH
plus
Mudhoney
Tickets £7.00
Wednesday 22nd March 1989
Kilburn National
234 Kilburn Road, NW6
DOORS OPEN 7.30PM
Nº 052

KILBURN NATIONAL BALLROOM
234, KILBURN HIGH ROAD
LONDON N.W.6.
AWAY FIXTURES
PRESENTS
SNUFF
PLUS
GUESTS
TUESDAY 27th NOVEMBER 1990
AT 7:30 P.M.
£ 4.00   TICKET No. 00017
TO BE RETAINED

THE JESUS AND MARY CHAIN
With Guests
HE SCIENTISTS   **Crime & the City Solution**
(Mon)   (Tues)
HEAD
Mon/Tues, 15/16th December, 7.30pm
NATIONAL BALLROOM

THE NATIONAL BALLROOM
234 KILBURN HIGH ROAD, NW6
MONDAY 15 DECEMBER
at 7.30 p.m.
Camouflage presents
JESUS & MARY CHAIN
Nº 564
TO BE RETAINED   NO RE-ADMISSION

The Mission
The National Ballroom
234, KILBURN HIGH ROAD, KILBURN, LONDON, N.W6.
Tuesday 20th February 1990
Doors 7.30pm   Show 8pm prompt
Tickets £3.00 advance
To be filmed for future broadcast
Nº 042

SNUFF
LEATHERFACE + WAT TYLER + midway still
THURSDAY,
15TH AUGUST
DOORS 7:00 PM
KILBURN
NATIONAL
BALLROOM
234 KILBURN
HIGH RD.
071-328-3141
£5 IN ADVANCE

New Roxy Theatre

Craven Park Road, Harlesden, NW10 8SH

Originally opened as the Odeon in 1937 with seating for over 1,600 people, it was eventually converted to the New Roxy Theatre music venue in 1976. The opening night was scheduled for Boxing Day 1976 the Sex Pistols, The Clash, The Damned and Johnny Thunders & the Heartbreakers all set to play as part of the Anarchy in the UK tour. Unfortunately the show was cancelled due to the controversy surrounding the Sex Pistols at the time. The bands had however previously used the New Roxy for rehearsals for the tour. Other bands such as Uriah Heap also used the venue for pre-tour rehearsals.

Acts to perform here during 1977 and 1978 include Sham 69, Girlschool, Steel Pulse, The Pleasers, Martha and The Vandellas, Three Degrees, Fatback Band, Mud, Junior Walker and the All Stars, The Clash, The Platters and The Supremes. Ray Smith, Flying Saucers and Warren Smith all played at The London Rock and Roll Festival here in 1978.

The building then became The Tara nightclub until 1986 and was demolished in 1989.

Since then a block of flats called Odeon Court occupy the space of the former venue.

Proud Camden

The Horse Hospital, The Stables Market, Chalk Farm Road, Camden, NW1 8AH

Situated in former stabling for lame horses from the adjacent railway goods depot, Proud Camden was founded in 2001 by art curator Alex Proud as a gallery space and bar by day, and a music venue during the evenings, although at weekends it often hosted all-day live music and late-night clubs.

Ed Sheeran played one his first ever performances here and a whole array of smaller bands played here. Proud also hosted well-known acts such as The Kooks, Supergrass, Jessie J, Kelis, Dizzee Rascal, ASAP Rocky, Calvin Harris and Feeder who all performed low-key shows here. Over the years there were also performances by Frank Turner, Role Models, Graham Coxon, The Crimea, Dirty Pretty Things, The Feeling, James, Robots in Disguise, Florence and the Machine, Babyshambles, Adam Ant, Martha Reeves and the Vandellas, Reverend and The Makers, Michael Monroe, Kunt and the Gang, Enter Shikari and Billy Bragg.

Hole were due to play a surprise gig in 2010 but cancelled at the last minute due to Courtney Love being blocked by police from leaving where she was staying in Park Lane due to what she described as a squatters' riot of 10,000 people partying in a neighbouring property.

Proud Camden closed in 2018 after the lease ended and landlord Camden Market said that they wanted fresh ideas for the site. The Horse Hospital is now occupied by FEST Camden, who describe themselves as "the nation's leading party venue!"

Purple Turtle

65 Crowndale Road, Camden, NW1 1TN

Situated in part of a former Post Office building close to Mornington Crescent station the Purple Turtle was a bar that was an active live music venue from 2003 to 2015 with bands playing most nights of the week.

Many up-and-coming unsigned bands of all genres played here such as Healthy Junkies, Ciccone, Rabies Babies, The King Blues and The Derellas. The venue sometimes hosted established acts including Meat Beat Manifesto, Inkubus Sukkubus, The Korgis, The Quireboys, David J, Richie Ramone, Senser, Walter Lure and Nicky Wire, who was promoting his solo album. The venue was well-known for being the best place in London for death, thrash and black metal gigs hosting frequent all-day events. Bands included such faves as Hellbastard, Fleshgod Apocalypse, Sold for Evil, Desecration and Basement Torture Killings. The venue was one used on the Camden Crawl (and later, Camden Rocks) annual mini festivals which operated at multiple venues simultaneously. One wristband enabled audience admission to all the venues.

The Purple Turtle closed down in 2015 with The Graveltones being the last band to play. It reopened the following year as The Crowndale with live music and a nightclub afterwards. The Kut, Towers of London and Hands Off Gretel were some of the bands that played during that brief period before it closed in 2017.

The premises are currently a nightclub called Favela.

143

Rainbow Theatre/Finsbury Park Astoria

232 Seven Sisters Road, Finsbury Park, N4 3NP

Arguably this is one of the most important places to feature in this volume of London's Lost Live Music Venues with many hundreds of household names playing here over its history.

The Finsbury Park Astoria opened as a cinema in 1930 with advertisements for the grand opening variety show gala claiming a seating capacity for 4,000 people. During the late 1950s and early 1960s, in common with many larger cinema venues, the by now 3,000 capacity Astoria also hosted live bands often with two shows per evening. The Beatles played 34 times between 1963 and 1965, many of those dates were part of their 1963 Christmas Shows along with Cilla Black and Rolf Harris. Chuck Berry, The Rolling Stones, Lulu, The Jimi Hendrix Experience, Sonny & Cher, The Animals, The Beach Boys and Ella Fitzgerald were some of the many acts to perform there during the 1960s. It was here in 1967 that Jimi Hendrix used lighter fuel and burnt his guitar onstage as he played and subsequently made it part of his act.

The venue was renamed the Odeon in 1970 and in 1971 The Byrds were the last band to play the cinema before it permanently moved over to hosting live music. It reopened as the Rainbow Theatre a couple of months later when The Who performed at the opening night having first appeared at the Astoria five years earlier. Later that year Frank Zappa was pushed off stage by a fan causing multiple fractures and in 1979 fans of The Clash smashed 200 seats. The Who returned in 1979 with new drummer Kenney Jones making his live debut for the band. Just about every touring act during the 1970s played the Rainbow with The Sensational Alex Harvey Band, AC/DC, The Clash, David Bowie, Van Halen, Sparks, Roxy Music, The Damned, Rainbow, The Police, Wings, Dolly Parton and The

Stranglers being just a few of the big names to play.

Recordings of concerts by Stiff Little Fingers, Genesis, Kool & the Gang, Focus, Van Morrison, T.Rex, Gary Glitter, Sweet, Ramones and Queen made their way onto live albums and there have been live video/DVD releases for Status Quo, Bob Marley & the Wailers, Yes, Foreigner and Thin Lizzy. The Rainbow was used in film scenes for Breaking Glass, The Great Rock 'n' Roll Swindle, Slade in Flame and Yanks.

Financial issues caused the closure of the Rainbow. The last ever concert there was by Elvis Costello and The Attractions on Christmas Eve in 1981. The building was largely disused apart from the odd boxing match before being taken over by the Universal Church of the Kingdom of God who still occupy the site.

The Regal/Sundown

6 Sterling Way, Edmonton, N18 2XZ

The Regal cinema opened in 1934 and had seating for 3,000 people with standing room for another 1,000. In the building there were also the Regal Rooms which had banqueting suites and a ballroom.

REGAL, EDMONTON
SUNDAY, JANUARY 24th 6 & 8.30 p.m.
ED. W. JONES presents
JOHNNY DANKWORTH ORCHESTRA
STAN STENNETT + KENNY BAKER QUARTET
3/- to 6/- (TOT 5223)

As well as showing films, orchestras including the Jack Parnell Band Show, the John Dankworth Big Band and Joe Loss and his Orchestra performed at the Regal during the 1950s. The decade also saw shows by Frank Sinatra, Paul Anka, Bob Cort's Skiffle Group and Bill Haley and His Comets. The performance by the latter in 1957 was the first ever rock and roll performance to be witnessed by Harry Webb who went on to change his name to Cliff Richard and return to perform with The Shadows at the Regal three times over the next few years. Jerry Lee Lewis made his UK debut here in 1958. His performance was shorter than anticipated and a press review of the gig commented that "he treats his audience with an attitude bordering on contempt". The 1960s saw live shows by The Animals, Little Richard, Chuck Berry, The Supremes and three dates by the Rolling Stones.

SUNDOWN EDMONTON N.18
FRIDAY 22nd DECEMBER 8.00pm
SUNDOWN BRIXTON S.W.9
SATURDAY 23rd DECEMBER 5.00pm and 8.30pm
TICKETS £1.25
Tickets in advance from theatre box offices
Edmonton 807-4649 Brixton 274-5482 and usual ticket agencies
Edwards and Edwards 734-9761 and London Theatre Bookings 437-1166

The Regal ceased to be a full-time cinema in 1972 and underwent an expensive conversion into the Sundown, part of a small chain of disco and live concert venues. Steppenwolf played the grand opening night and many other popular, mainly rock acts, of the period played here including Hawkwind, Heavy Metal Kids, Humble Pie, Electric Light Orchestra, Elton John, T.Rex, Curved Air and Lou Reed. The Faces played seven dates here and The Who also played the venue four times.

146

This Sundown club lasted longer than its Mile End counterpart but still only lasted until early 1974 when the Regal Cinema reopened, using seating that had remained in situ in the circle. This too was short lived and within a year it had been become a bingo hall, which survived until the building was demolished in 1985.

A new building on the site is currently occupied by a Lidl supermarket and the United Church of the Kingdom of God. One small consolation is that a memory of the Regal lives on in a modern mosaic on the side of the building and old signage for the Regal Rooms remains visible on an adjacent building.

Royal Ballroom

415-419 High Road, Tottenham, N17 6RD

This was originally built as a roller skating rink which opened in 1910 which was soon refitted as a cinema. The cinema had closed by 1925 and was converted into the Tottenham Palais dance hall where the likes of Archie Alexander and his band provided the big band jazz.

During the 1950s it was renamed the Tottenham Royal and by the 1960s started hosting popular chart acts. Local boys Dave Clark Five played here 12 times early in 1964 whilst enjoying chart success with their hits, which all featured their self-styled "Tottenham Sound" in response to Liverpool's Mersey Beat. Later on in the decade The Who, Status Quo, Marmalade, Small Faces, Desmond Dekker, Arthur Conley and Prince Buster all played here. Amen Corner released a live album of one of their gigs recorded here in 1969 (The National Welsh Coast Live Explosion Company LP) and in 1973 David Bowie rehearsed here for a week prior to the Ziggy Stardust US tour. Sweet, The New Seekers and Wizzard played here in the early 1970s and resident groups continued to perform at dances as well as better known acts including The Nolan Sisters, Joe Brown and The Bruvvers and The Barron Knights. The Royal was also popular for its DJ nights playing reggae and soul music.

The Royal became The Mayfair in 1979 where Queen, Elvis Costello and The Attractions and The Prodigy played concerts before the venue was renamed The Ritzy a few years, and then later The Zone, the United Nations Club and finally The Temple before it was demolished in 2004. The site is now a block of flats with shops on the ground floor.

MECCA DANCING
ROYAL
★★★★★★★★★
TOTTENHAM

FRIDAY 29th SEPT.
THE
SMALL FACES

FRIDAY 6th OCT. 7·30–11·30
Simon Dupree
& the Big Sound
PLUS TWO RESIDENT BANDS

76
No advance tickets
will be issued
ALL pay at
the door

Royalty Ballroom

Rear of Dennis Parade, Winchmore Hill Road, Southgate, N14 6AA

The Royalty was a large dancehall at the back of a parade of shops. In the late 1960s it hosted live performances by Family, Savoy Brown, The All Night Workers and Mungo Jerry.

The Royalty is fondly remembered by the Rockabilly scene for its Thursday nights between 1978 and 1981 with flyers billing itself as "the home of rock 'n' roll". The venue hosted acts such as Don Everly, The Meteors, Matchbox, Bo Diddley, The Polecats, Carl Perkins, Crazy Cavan and the Rhythm Rockers, and The Deltas. Bill Haley and the Comets played in one of their final UK appearances before he passed away. A 1980 film Blue Suede Shoes, a documentary about the revival of British rock n' roll, shows footage from The Royalty. During the same period weekends at The Royalty were influential in the soul and jazz-funk scene with DJs such as Froggy, Gregg Edwards, Robbie Vincent and Pete Tong. This scene was featured in a TV show called 20th Century Box with Danny Baker presenting a piece about the beginnings of the jazz funk scene in and around London.

For many people the most memorable appearance of The Royalty on screen is when the interior was used for scenes in the 1979 film Quadrophenia, where Jimmy (Phil Daniels) upstages Ace (Sting) by leaping from the balcony of a Brighton dance hall.

In 1981 there was also a club night called Rox where The Higsons, Fad Gadget, Bananarama, Shakatak and Department S played live sets. By 1983 the venue was the called the Pink Elephant and mainly played pre-recorded music although Break Machine and Forrest came to perform their hits live here. The former venue is now a gym.

150

Perry Haines
PRESENTS

DEPARTMENT S.
GO BANANAS OVER
Bananarama
with
D.J. STEVE LEWIS
SATURDAY, 5th DECEMBER
DOORS OPEN AT 8.00 p.m.

JETS & SHARKS
WELCOME
FREE MEMBERSHIP
GET UP · GET DOWN
GET HEP

ROX
THE ROYALTY SOUTHGATE

★ THE *Royalty* NITESPOT ★
HOME OF 'ROCK 'N' ROLL

AUGUST 7th   CRAZY CAVAN
14th   ROCKIN' LOUIE, and THE MAMMA JAMMERS
                    plus SHOTGUN

21st   **RAY CAMPI · RHYTHM HAWKS**
                    TICKET £2.00

28th   *Buzz and the Flyers*
              Polecats   TICKET £2.00

SEPTEMBER 4th   FLYING SAUCERS

ROYALTY NITESPOT, Winchmore Hill Road, Southgate N.14
TELEPHONE: 01-886 4112
OFF. SOUTHGATE UNDERGROUND STATION (PICC. LINE)

ROYALTY

ROX INTO '82

SAT 30th JAN

SHAKATAK
with 200 MPH Dance Music Man
FROGGY

ROX
LONDON'S NEW DANCE CLUB
EVERY SATURDAY
ROYALTY SOUTHGATE N14
1 min Southgate Und. Stn.
Tel. 01-886 4112

ROYALTY BALLROOM, SOUTHGATE
(1 min. Southgate Underground)
LIVE GROUPS
Every Tuesday Night
THIS TUESDAY, JUNE 6th
Don't be alone out there — hear the

SOUND SET
Licensed Bars   8.00 - 11.00   5/- at door

ROYALTY BALLROOM, SOUTHGATE
(1 min. Southgate Underground)
THIS TUESDAY, AUGUST 8th
THE FANTASTIC
COLOURED RAISINS SHOW
FEATURING
KING OSSIE, HONEY DARLING and EARL GREENE
Licensed Bars   8.00-11.00 p.m.

CHRIS THOMPSON, GROUCHO + STEVE
ADMISSION FREE EVERY NIGHT

Royalty SOUTHGATE
"LONDON'S MUSIC NITE SPOT"
This Friday, 24th June
U.S.A. recording stars
THE MARVELS
This Saturday 25th June
Sally James with Billy Ocean and Guests
WINCHMORE HILL ROAD, SOUTHGATE, N.14
(Opposite Southgate Underground)
Telephone: 01-886 4112

151

Screen on the Green

83 Upper Street, Islington, N1 0NP

The Screen on The Green is a small single screen cinema that originally opened as the Empress Electric Theatre in 1913. It is one of the oldest continuously running cinemas in the UK.

There are no records of any live music at this venue before a punk showcase gig organised by Malcolm McLaren in 1976. The Sex Pistols headlined the gig which was billed as a Midnight Special and was set to close at dawn. Support was provided by The Clash and Buzzcocks who were making their London debut. The Sex Pistols returned the following year for their first live performance with new bass player Sid Vicious. The support band at that gig was The Slits. In 2013 Viv Albertine of The Slits and Glen Matlock of the Sex Pistols returned to play the venue as part of a 100-Year Celebration of the Screen on the Green and a tribute to the Midnight Special.

A handful of other acts have performed over the years at Screen on the Green at one-off live events. These include This Heat, Hard Corps, The Antlers and The Human Condition. Due to modernisation since the first gig in 1976 the capacity has dropped from 600 to now just 120 partly due to the addition of an internal foyer and luxury seating.

The venue is now called Everyman Screen on the Green and remains a cinema open to the public as well as being available for private events.

Three Horseshoes

28 Heath Street, Hampstead, NW3 6TE

The upstairs former billiard room of The Three Horseshoes pub became a significant venue on the London folk club circuit during the 1960s.

Martin Carthy in his band The Three City Four, The Tinkers and The Exiles all had residencies at the Three Horseshoes Folk Club at various times during the decade, usually supporting visiting acts such as John Martyn, Ralph McTell, Paul Simon, Strawbs, Sandy Denny and Roy Harper. David Bowie played two solo lunchtime shows in 1969 two months before the release of his 'Space Oddity' single. One of the performances was recorded and four songs have since appeared on the A Letter to Hermione bootleg CD.

Since the early 1970s the upstairs room has been a theatre called The Pentameters. As well as plays the theatre has hosted many comedians at the start of their careers including Alexei Sayle, Jasper Carrott, Adrian Edmondson and Ben Elton. The ground floor pub later became a branch of JD Wetherspoon until 2005 and the new owners renamed the pub as The Horseshoe which became the birthplace of Camden Town Brewery when the landlord started brewing below the pub. A hanging sign by the entrance proclaiming "David Bowie played here" has long since disappeared.

TINKERS CLUB, Three Horseshoes, Heath St., by Hampstead Underground. One of America's best folksong writers and recording artists, **PAUL SIMON** and **THE TINKERS.**

SOUTH EAST

ABC Croydon

225 London Road, Croydon, CR0 2AZ

This cinema opened as The Savoy Cinema in 1936 and was then renamed the ABC Croydon in 1958 after a refurbishment with seating for over 2,000 people. The cinema hosted live concerts mainly between 1962 and 1967. The Beatles played here in 1963, on the day before their first album Please Please Me was released. Other acts to perform here during that period included Vanilla Fudge, Brian Poole and The Tremeloes, Cliff Richard and The Shadows, Helen Shapiro, Billy Fury, Gerry and the Pacemakers, The Animals, Carl Perkins, Cilla Black and The Dave Clark Five. PJ Proby performed here in 1965 when the seam

of his velvet trousers split at the crotch while on stage causing a nationwide scandal in the press. This incident led to bans on PJ Proby appearances by the theatre chains and BBC TV and Proby's UK career lost momentum as a result.

Spooky Tooth played here in 1969 as did Deep Purple in 1971. Archive records suggest that they were two of the last concerts here before the cinema was split into a three-screen cinema in 1972. It was renamed the Canon in 1986 though that closed down in 1996 due to competition from a new multiplex opening nearby. The cinema then ran as an independent cinema called the Safari showing mainly Bollywood films until its closure in 2004. It was finally demolished in 2007 and replaced by flats and shops.

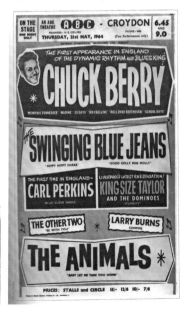

Bal Tabarin

435 Downham Way, Downham, Bromley, BR1 5EW

The Bal Tabarin was a large dance hall at the back of the Downham Tavern built in 1930 as part of a large new London County Council housing estate. The 1956 edition of The Guinness Book of Records listed the Downham Tavern as the largest public house in the world with two bars each able to hold 1,000 people serving up to 130,000 bottles of beer on holiday weekends.

Named after a Parisian cabaret club, the Bal Tabarin during the 1960s hosted afternoon bingo sessions several days a week and dances and jazz performances by the likes of Acker Bilk, Humphrey Lyttleton and Ken Colyer during the evenings. Between 1967 and 1969 there were pop, rock and blues bands, sometimes promoted by the Downham Folk Club. Acts to play here included Cream, The Who, Procol Harum, Geno Washington and the Ram Jam Band, The Crazy World of Arthur Brown, Gasworks and The Herd. Radio Caroline sponsored a show in May 1967 headlined by The Riot Squad, whose bassist had switched to lead vocals after David Bowie had left the band earlier in the month. Bowie did appear at the Folk Club two years later when he performed there as a favour for his friend for a £5 fee. The gig was packed as 'Space Oddity' had recently been a chart hit.

The Bal Tabarin had a brief return to hosting live bands in 1988 when The

Lords of the New Church, Dr. Feelgood, Sonny Burgess and Shy played here. In 1989, it held the Weekend of The Long Knives event, a psychobilly festival featuring around 30 bands including The Stingrays, Meteors and Guana Batz. The hall also hosted boxing events and all-day raves around that period.

The land was purchased by a supermarket chain during the 1990s and the pub and its hall were demolished. A supermarket, car park and a smaller Downham Tavern have since been built on the site.

BAL TABARIN BALLROOM

ADJ TO THE DOWNHAM TAVERN. DOWNHAM WAY, BROMLEY

THURSDAY 13TH OCTOBER
STOCKTONS WING
ADM £6.00

Plus YABBA DABBA DOO CLUB every Friday CREDIT CARD BOOKINGS. Open all hours (01) 379 4444 BKG FEE.
FORTHCOMING ATTRACTION: THE WOLFE TONES OCT 30TH.
Doors open 7pm 'til late each night. Buses to the door: 36b, 124,141, or 885.
Nearest station: Grove Park BR.

BAL TABARIN BALLROOM

ADJ TO THE DOWNHAM TAVERN. DOWNHAM WAY, BROMLEY

SATURDAY 26TH/SUNDAY 27TH NOVEMBER
ALBERT LEE
(AMERICAN GUITAR LEGEND)
+ SPECIAL GUEST ADM £7.00

CREDIT CARD BOOKINGS. Open all hours (01) 379 4444 BKG FEE.
Doors open 7pm 'til late each night. Buses to the door: 36b, 124, 141, or
N85. Nearest station: Grove Park BR.

BAL TABARIN BALLROOM

ADJ TO THE DOWNHAM TAVERN. DOWNHAM WAY, BROMLEY

ONLY LONDON DATE
SATURDAY 12TH NOVEMBER
GUANA BATZ
+ THE EJITS
ADM £4.50

CREDIT CARD BOOKINGS. Open all hours (01) 379 4444 BKG FEE.
Doors open 7pm 'til late each night. Buses to the door: 36b, 124,141, or N85.
Nearest station: Grove Park BR.

BAL TABARIN BALLROOM

ADJ TO THE DOWNHAM TAVERN. DOWNHAM WAY, BROMLEY

THURSDAY 22ND DECEMBER
(ONLY LONDON DATE)
DR FEELGOOD
CHRISTMAS PARTY
+ MEAN RED SPIDER

TEL NO'S: 698 6507, 695 5097. CREDIT CARD BOOKINGS. Open all hours (01) 379 4444 BKG FEE.
Doors open 7pm 'til late each night. Buses to the door: 36b, 124,141, or N85.
Nearest station: Grove Park BR.

BAL TABARIN BALLROOM

ADJ TO THE DOWNHAM TAVERN. DOWNHAM WAY, BROMLEY

SATURDAY 3RD DECEMBER
THE FLYING PICKETS
+ SUPPORT ADM £5.00

CREDIT CARD BOOKINGS. Open all hours (01) 379 4444 BKG FEE.
Doors open 7pm 'til late each night. Buses to the door: 36b, 124,141, or
N85. Nearest station: Grove Park BR.

ONLY LONDON DATE
DR FEELGOOD
+ WILD FRONTIERS
FRIDAY 29TH JULY
TICKETS £5.50 (Advance) £6.00 (On Night)
GLITTER BAND
+ ROOMATES
£4.50 (Advance) £5.00 (on night)
FRIDAY 5TH AUGUST
LORDS OF THE NEW CHURCH
AUGUST 11th

**THE BAL TABARIN BALLROOM
THE DOWNHAM TAVERN,
DOWNHAM WAY, BROMLEY**
(BOX OFF 695 5099) 698 6507 695 5097

THE CHRISTMAS PSYCOBILLY PARTY
FRIDAY 23RD DECEMBER,
5pm TILL LATE

BAL-TABARIN BALLROOM BROMLEY
01-695 5099

METEORS
+ RESTLESS + DEMENTED ARE GO
+ LONG TALL TEXANS
+ COFFIN NAILS + MIDHITERS
+ TURNPIKE CRUISERS
+ SURFIN' WOMBATZ
+ OTHER ATTRACTIONS £7

SUPERB VENUE – 20 MINS LONDON
ENQUIRIES·TRANSPORT·TICKETS
01-289 0779

Space Oddity

Adm. 6/-

Folk Club,
Downham Tavern,
nham, Bromley, Kent.
141, 124.
Grove Park Stn.

The Black Prince

Southwold Road, Bexley, DA5 1ND

The Black Prince, a large pub with a dining room offering overnight accommodation, was built in 1934. It was named after the son of King Edward III and local lore is that there is a ghost of him in his black armour at nearby Hall Place where he stayed en route to fight a war with France.

The Bexley Jazz Club
AT THE
BLACK PRINCE HOTEL

RHYTHM AND BLUES CLUB EVERY SUNDAY

Sunday, 9th ,,	THE TIMEBOX
	From U.S.A.—A Giant of the blues
Sunday, 16th ,,	FREDDY KING
Sunday, 23rd ,,	CLIFF BENNETT
Sunday, 30th ,,	COLOURED RAISINS
Sunday, 7th Dec.	THE DAVE AMBOY SHOW
Sunday, 14th ,,	FERRIS WHEEL
Sunday, 21st ,,	THE PEDDLERS

MONDAY NIGHT IS JAZZ NIGHT

Monday, 10th ,,	ERIC SILK
Monday, 17th ,,	BRIAN GREEN
Monday, 24th ,,	ALEX WELSH
Monday, 1st Dec.	CHRIS BARBER
Monday, 8th ,,	SAMMY REMMINGTON
Monday, 15th ,,	ALEXANDERS JAZZBAND
Monday, 22nd ,,	BILL NILES

The Black Prince was a popular live music venue from 1964 with many appearances that year by the Graham Bond Organisation. Bands who played between 1965 until the end of the decade included The Action, Steampacket, Geno Washington and The Ram Jam Band, the Moody Blues, Cliff Bennett and The Rebel Rousers, Brian Auger and Julie Driscoll, The Long John Baldry Show and Jimmy Cliff. The 1965 South-Eastern Jazz and Blues Festival all-dayer was held here with one stage in the usual hall and one in in the grounds. Solomon Burke, Zoot Money, Unit 4 Plus 2, Spencer Davis Group, Downliners Sect and DJs from Radio Caroline all appeared at the festival. Eric Clapton was scheduled to play his last ever gig with John Mayall's Bluesbreakers at the Black Prince in 1966, although according to Dave Thomson's book Cream: How Eric Clapton Took the World by Storm, he was fired early and replaced by Peter Green for this gig.

During the early 1970s acts who played here included Mungo Jerry, Fusion Orchestra, Holy Mackerel, Stealers Wheel, Roxy Music, Status Quo, Genesis, Supertramp, Uriah Heep, Hawkwind, The Groundhogs and Faces billed as The Faces featuring Rod Stewart. By 1974 the live music had wound down and was replaced by discos.

These days the building is a Holiday Inn with substantial hotel wings attached. The Black Prince name survives only in the adjacent roundabout which provides access to the A2.

THE BLACK PRINCE CLUB
BEXLEY, KENT

SUN. 23rd JAN.	**ARGENT**	*plus REFUGEE*
„ 30th JAN.	**'GENESIS'**	
„ 6th FEB.	**'IF'** *plus JUDE*	
„ 13th FEB.	**'LINDISFARNE'**	
„ 26th FEB.	**'SKID ROW'**	
„ 27th FEB.	**'STRAY'**	

HOLY MACKEREL
ON THE ROAD
DECEMBER

6th:	Dundee Technical College
7th:	Glasgow University
8th:	Sunderland Polytechnic
9th:	Hilltop Club, Carlisle
10th:	Tavern, Dorchester
11th:	Weymouth College of Ed.
12th:	Tricorn, Portsmouth
14th:	Stoneground, Manchester
16th:	Brooklyn Tech, Birmingham
17th:	Black Prince, Bexley

Reception   Holiday Inn

The Black Prince

Borough Hall

179-183 London Road, Croydon CR0 2RJ

This was part of the Greenwich Town Hall complex built in 1939 and was described by Nikolaus Pevsner, the architectural historian, as "the only town hall of any London borough to represent the style of our time adequately".

During the early 1960s, Borough Hall, a wing of the Town Hall, hosted dances and the Twist Club, a popular venue for Mods. The Rolling Stones played an early gig here in 1963 and while having a drink in the bar the band learned that President Kennedy had been killed. David Jones (later known as Bowie) was at the show who later said that Jagger's onstage interaction that night with the audience really confirmed to him that he wanted to be a rock star. A heckler shouted, "Git yer 'air cut!", to which Jagger retaliated: "What and look like you?!" The High Numbers played here four times in 1964 and once again in 1965 as The Who. Cliff Bennett and The Rebel Rousers, Downliners Sect, The Kinks and The Yardbirds also played there around this period.

In 1965 the local borough was merged with neighbouring Woolwich to form the London Borough of Greenwich with its new headquarters at Woolwich Town Hall. The old Town Hall continued to be used for gigs and dances and Status Quo, Soft Machine, Sweet, Budgie, Badfinger, 10CC, Clannad, Ralph McTell, Labi Siffre have all played here over the years.

A plaque celebrates local band Squeeze who played an early gig here in 1975. Two members of the band were present at the unveiling of the plaque in 2010 and afterwards they played an acoustic set in the Hall. The plaque disappeared soon afterwards but has since been replaced.

The building was later occupied by the Greenwich Dance Agency until 2018 and has been empty, apart from a brief occupation by squatters, ever since. Proposals have been submitted for a refurbishment of the building to reopen it as a theatre.

Invitation

to a

Disco

(by Innovation)

at

Greenwich Borough Hall,
Royal Hill, Greenwich

Live Music

by

'Squeeze'

On Friday 25th April, 1975
between 7.00 p.m. -
12.00 p.m.

Admission 45p

Bar available,
No admittance after
10.00 p.m.

Proceeds in aid of
Inverclever Lodge Trust.

Greenwich Borough Hall
ROYAL HILL, SE10

CLANNAD

FRIDAY
JANUARY 31
Evening 8.00

Greenwich Entertainment Service presents

CLANNAD
Plus
FREDDIE WHITE

Friday 31st January 1986 at 8pm
Greenwich Borough Hall · Royal Hill · Greenwich SE10
Tickets £6 · £5 (£5 · £4 Concessions and Students)

Available from
Greenwich Entertainment Service · 25 Woolwich New Road · Woolwich SE18
Advance Bookings 01-317 8687 · Credit Cards 01-855 5900
Greenwich Theatre Box-office · Crooms Hill · SE10 (Personal Callers) and at the door

GREENWICH LEISURE

GREENWICH BOROUGH HALL
ROYAL HILL, S.E.10

FRIDAY
9th NOV.
at 8 p.m.

IN CONCERT

MUNGO JERRY

PLUS SUPPORTING GROUP

TICKETS: 50p, 75p & £1. AVAILABLE FROM:
25 WOOLWICH NEW ROAD, S.E.18. TEL: 854 5250

Borough Hall

165

Cable

33 Bermondsey Street, London Bridge, SE1 3JW

Cable opened in 2009 and like the nearby SeOne was situated under the railway arches of London Bridge Station. The club was awarded Time Out magazine's "Best Club Venue" in 2011.

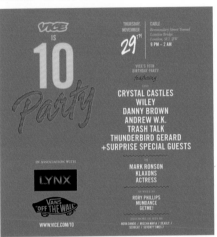

The club with a crowd capacity of around 1,000 people was best known for DJs playing house, techno and electro, through to grime, drum and bass and dubstep. However live acts did occasionally perform at Cable. Venetian Snares played in 2010 and the same year there was the London Twestival, a global charity festival organised entirely via Twitter, where Kal Lavelle and She Makes War played. In 2012 Crystal Castles, Wiley, Andrew W.K. and Iggy Azalea played at the 10th anniversary party for the British edition of Vice magazine with Mark Ronson and Klaxons DJing the event. Singer Cari Golden and experimental rock band Ultraísta both played events here in 2012.

Cable closed abruptly in 2013 after the landlord took possession of the premises to accommodate rebuilding and modernisation of the adjacent station. Unlike SeOne, the original arch housing Cable still exists but an emergency staircase from the station is now situated inside the former club.

Chislehurst Caves

Caveside Close, Old Hill, Chislehurst, BR7 5NL

The caves at Chislehurst, a leafy suburb in South East London, are a labyrinth of over 20 miles of man-made tunnels, dug over a period of 8,000 years. The caves were dug for chalk used in lime burning and brick making as well as for flints to fire tinderboxes and flintlock guns. Munitions were stored here for the Woolwich Arsenal in the First World War and then mushrooms were grown there in the 1920 and 1930s. During the Second World War they were used as an air-raid shelter protecting over 15,000 people every night during the Blitz.

The caves were used as a music venue from the 1950s when the South London Jazz Club organised concerts featuring jazz musicians such as Kenny Ball, Acker Bilk and Humphrey Littleton and skiffle acts including Lonnie Donegan. During the 1960s acts playing here

included Davie Jones and The King Bees, Eric Burdon and The Animals, The Jimi Hendrix Experience, Them, Pink Floyd, The Yardbirds, The Herd, The Rolling Stones and The Spencer Davis Group.

Led Zeppelin hired the Caves in 1974 for the lavish launch party of their Swansong record label when Roy Harper, John Chilton's Feetwarmers and George Melly played to an audience including Bad Company, The Pretty Things, Bob Harris and Marianne Faithfull along with an assortment of press and industry types. The party had drink servers dressed as nuns, fire-breathers, a woman lying down in a coffin completely naked while covered in jelly, and naked male wrestlers. Bands to play here later in the 1970s included Menace, Pere Ubu and The Slits. The Stingrays, The Meteors, The Prisoners, Hepatitis Risk and CASE played here in the 1980s

167

and The Primitives played five nights in 1992.

The caves have appeared in Doctor Who in 1972 (The Mutants) and music videos for metal bands Iron Maiden ('Can I Play with Madness') and Cradle of Filth ('Honey and Sulphur').

Health and safety issues mean that gigs can no longer take place at the Chislehurst Caves. The caves are open as a tourist attraction with guided tours offered to the public.

CHISLEHURST CAVES
next to Chislehurst Station
1st BIRTHDAY
This Saturday, May 3. 7.30 p.m.
ALL BRITAIN SCOOP!
For the very first time at any Jazz Club
ESQUIRE RECORDS'

THE HAPPY WANDERERS

direct from their tour of the West End.

Usual supporting groups, etc., etc.
AND BRING YOUR OWN CANDLE
to London's most unusual Jazz Club,

CHISLEHURST CAVES
Saturday
19th Nov
Adm £1.00
THE SLITS
+ THE TICKETS
8-12
BAR
Tickets in advance from Bonaparte Records, Bromley; Music Town, Sidcup

3/6.
CHISLEHURST CAVES
(next to Chislehurst Station) 7.30:
1, 2, 3,
4, 5, 6,
7!
7 CHEERS FOR
GRAHAM STEWART'S SEVEN
on our main stage tonight. Under the **ULTRA-VIOLET**, the Hard Travellers. Also seven supporting groups. All types of candles permitted.—See also Tuesday.

CHISLEHURST CAVES
(next to Chislehurst Station), 7.30:
DANGER!
THERE'S A FIRE DOWN BELOW
KINDLED BY
GRAHAM STEWART'S SEVEN
and fanned by
SEVEN SUPPORTING GROUPS.
TO ADD TO THE HEAT.
BRING YOUR OWN CANDLE!

Cinatra's/Top Rank/

169 London Road, Croydon, CR0 2RJ

The Top Rank was billed by their owners as "one of the biggest ballrooms in the South of England" when it opened as part of the 1960s Zodiac development which also included housing, offices and shops.

The venue laid on dinner dances with house bands three nights a week plus concerts by popular visiting artists who, during the late 1960s, included The Equals, Love Affair, Booker T. and The M.G.'s, Curtis Mayfield and Jimmy Ruffin. In 1967 a band called 1984 won the area finals of a nationwide talent contest held here. The guitarist of that band was Brian May who later enjoyed even greater success with Queen. The early 1970s saw performances by Eddie Floyd, The Crystals, Slade, Pink Fairies, Manfred Mann's Earth Band, Colosseum, Bob Marley and The Wailers, and Al Green.

The Top Rank closed in 1974 and reopened in 1976 as Cinatra's with cabaret nights featuring live appearances from stars such as Max Bygraves. During the 1980s Cinatra's was used for filming the Unforgettable live television music show on Channel Four. The show, produced by the club's owner, focused on contemporary performances by artists in the latter stages of their careers. These included The Glitter Band, Mud, Dave Dee, Dozy, Beaky, Mick and Tich, Joe Brown, Del Shannon, The New Seekers, The Ivy League, The Nashville Teens and PJ Proby. The most unforgettable episode was in 1983, which turned out to be Billy Fury's last ever public performance before he died of a heart attack a few days later. During the 1990s Cinatra's was a popular nightclub though as the years progressed its reputation gradually declined. It eventually closed in 2004 and the building remains derelict. The adjoining housing block's claim to fame is that TV sitcom Peep Show, starring David Mitchell and Robert Webb, was filmed on location for the first two series in one of the flats.

The Coronet Theatre

28 New Kent Road, Elephant and Castle, SE1 6TJ

The Coronet was originally opened in 1879 as the Elephant and Castle Theatre where the young locally born Charlie Chaplin is believed to have performed. The Theatre is featured in the short 1926 documentary London After Dark. It was converted to a cinema in 1932 and later renamed the ABC in 1966 with metal panels erected to conceal the original features of the exterior. It became the Coronet Cinema in 1981 which closed down in 1999.

The derelict building was refurbished and relaunched as The Coronet Theatre in 2003 as a nightclub hosting many performances by well-known artists including Justin Timberlake, Oasis, The Orb, Franz Ferdinand, Primal Scream, Blur, Heaven 17, The Fall, Florence and the Machine, Hawkwind, The Rifles and Black Lips. In 2014 Tom Jones, Peter Gabriel, David Gilmore and Ronan Keating performed at a private party at the Coronet. A Peter and Test Tube Babies gig was recorded and released as a live DVD called Keep Britain Untidy. In 2015 The Maccabees made a documentary called Elephant Days, about recording their album in Elephant and Castle, and also had their album launch party at The Coronet. The Coronet also hosted many DJ nights along with occasional boxing and wrestling bouts. During 2015 there was a stabbing and gun incident at the venue resulting in the council temporarily banning urban music.

Two years later a fight broke out and missiles were thrown as hundreds of people rushed the front door of a 2,500-strong rave which featured sets from up to 20 DJs playing hip-hop, house and bashment music, descended into chaos.

The venue closed at the beginning of 2018 and the building was demolished in 2021 as part of a major regeneration project for the area.

Crystal Palace Hotel

2 Anerley Hill, Upper Norwood, SE19 2AA

This venue has hosted live music since the 1960s. Its most prolific year that decade was 1969 when Percy Sledge, Arthur Conley, Inez And Charlie Foxx, Prince Buster, The Equals, Chicken Shack and Ben E. King all performed. Fleetwood Mac played here twice that year despite playing more high-profile gigs at the Royal Albert Hall around the same period. The venue became popular again during the mod revival of 1979-1980 when The Small Hours, Squire, The Merton Parkas, The Lambrettas, The Circles and Purple Hearts all played. Around that time there were also gigs by The Associates, Stray Cats, Phil Daniels and The Cross, The Soft Boys, Q-Tips and Wasted Youth.

The venue's name changed to The Sportsman and finally The Grape and Grain which continued to put on blues and jazz bands right up to its closure in 2017.

At the time of writing the pub remains boarded up but there are plans by pub company J.D Wetherspoon to reopen the pub as The Royal Crystal Palace.

Crystal Palace National Sports Centre

Ledrington Road, SE19 2BB

Crystal Palace National Sports Centre is an athletics stadium opened in 1964 in Crystal Palace Park on the site of a football ground which hosted the FA Cup final from 1895 to 1914.

The stadium was used for major concerts between 1993 and 2005 with a varying crowd capacity of up to 44,000 people. Headliners to play one-day events include Depeche Mode, The Beautiful South, Paul Weller, Santana and The Sex Pistols. Coldplay and Bruce Springsteen played two dates each. Supporting acts at events over the years included The Sisters of Mercy, Travis, Interpol, Dropkick Murphys, Supergrass, The Libertines, UB40, Blue, Texas, Teenage Fanclub and Republica.

The stadium used to hold international athletics events before the new London Stadium opened in Stratford for the 2012 Olympics. Concerts are no longer held here amid concerns that the stadium needs significant investment to secure its future as a community facility.

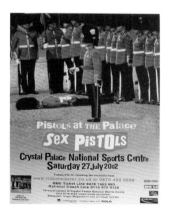

Davis Theatre

73 High Street, Croydon, CR0 1QE

The Davis Theatre built in 1928 was, at the time, the second largest cinema to be built in England with seating for 3,700 people. The elaborately constructed theatre was equipped to show films and host ballet and stage productions.

The London Philharmonic Orchestra played here in 1939 and in 1944 a wartime bomb killed six audience members though only caused minimal damage to the theatre. It reopened soon after the war with the inaugural performance of the Royal Philharmonic Orchestra in 1946. In the 1950s there were world-class concerts by Frankie Laine, Maurice Chevalier, Johnnie Ray, Eartha Kitt, Paul Anka, Louis Armstrong, Mario Lanza, Count Basie, Gracie Fields and Liberace. Rock and roll arrived in Croydon when Bill Haley and his Comets played the Davis Theatre for two nights in 1957. The local paper reported that police would be on duty inside and outside the venue should Haley's fans decide to repeat a riot that occurred when he arrived at Waterloo Station a few days beforehand. Buddy Holly and The Crickets, Cliff Richard and Guy Mitchell also played here during the late 1950s.

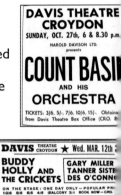

TOUR - OCTOBER 1956

LIBERACE
GEORGE LIBERACE
AND
THE GEORGE MELACHRINO CONCERT ORCHESTRA

Royal Festival Hall **LONDON**	October 1st at 8 p.m.	
The De Montfort Hall **LEICESTER**	October 3rd at 7 p.m.	
The Davis Theatre **CROYDON**	October 7th at 3 p.m.	
Belle Vue **MANCHESTER**	October 8th at 7.30 p.m.	
City Hall **SHEFFIELD**	October 11th at 7 p.m.	
Theatre Royal **DUBLIN**	October 13th at 3 p.m.	
Royal Albert Hall **LONDON**	October 15th at 7.30 p.m. October 17th at 7.30 p.m.	

The Davis Theatre closed down in 1959 with the last live concert being Jazz at the Philharmonic with Ella Fitzgerald and the Gene Kupra Quartet. The main part of the building was demolished soon afterwards. An office block called Davis House now occupies the site. A plaque details the history of the former Theatre and during its unveiling in 2004 the chairman of the Cinema Theatre Association commented that the Davies Theatre is "possibly the greatest architectural loss Croydon has sustained".

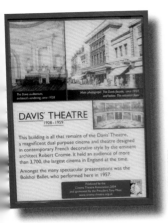

DAVIS' THEATRE
1928 - 1959

This building is all that remains of the Davis' Theatre, a magnificent dual purpose cinema and theatre designed in contemporary French decorative style by the eminent architect Robert Cromie. It held an audience of more than 3,700, the largest cinema in England at the time.

Amongst the many spectacular presentations was the Bolshoi Ballet, who performed here in 1957.

IN THE
DAVIS THEATRE
WHICH STOOD ON THIS SITE
SIR THOMAS BEECHAM BtCH
CONDUCTED THE
FIRST PERFORMANCE OF THE
ROYAL PHILHARMONIC ORCHESTRA
ON
SUNDAY 15th SEPTEMBER
1946

DAVIS THEATRE, CROYDON · SUNDAY, SEPTEMBER 27
5.30 and 8 p.m.
ED. W. JONES PRESENTS LAST APPEARANCE IN THIS COUNTRY OF
★ **BILLY DANIELS** ★
WITH FULL SUPPORTING COMPANY
3/- to 7/6   CROYDON 3300

Granada Dartford

30 Spital Street, Dartford, DA1 2DL

Just a mile away from the border with the London Borough of Bexley is the former State Cinema in Dartford, which opened in 1935 with seating for 1,500 people.

It was re-named the Granada in 1949 and as with many Granada Cinemas from the late 1950s it also began to stage live acts as well as show films. These were generally in the form of touring rock 'n' roll package tours with numerous acts on the bill often with two shows per evening. Cliff Richard and The Shadows and Petula Clark played here in 1959 and between 1960 and 1964 acts that graced the stage included The Hollies, Billy J. Kramer and The Dakotas, Duffy Power, Rolf Harris, Marty Wilde, Joe Brown and The Bruvvers, Billy Fury, Adam Faith, Tommy Steele, Gene Vincent, Johnny Kidd and The Pirates, Cliff Bennett and The Rebel Rousers,

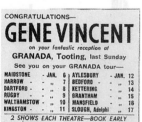

Helen Shapiro, The Bachelors and The John Barry Seven. John Barry became better known later for composing the scores for 11 James Bond themes. Surprisingly, despite some members of The Rolling Stones and The Pretty Things growing up in the area neither band ever played at the Granada.

The cinema was converted into a bingo club in 1975 and closed in 2014. These days the building is owned by Net Church, part of the Evangelical Alliance and Assemblies of God UK.

Granada Dartford

Granada Tooting

50 Mitcham Road, Tooting, SW17 9NA

The Granada opened in 1931 and at the time it was considered by many to be one of the most spectacular cinemas in the UK. It was designed by the cinema and theatre architect Cecil A. Massey for Sidney Bernstein, as part of his Granada cinema chain. The interior was by the Russian theatre designer Theodore Komisarjevsky. Despite having over 3,000 seats over 2,000 people were turned away for a packed opening ceremony featuring a performance by trumpeters from The Life Guards and tunes played on the cinema's Wurlitzer organ.

As with many others in this chain of cinemas the Granada in Tooting was important as a local venue for live music and wrestling. The 1950s saw performances by Johnnie Ray, Frank Sinatra, Max Bygraves, Cliff Richard and The Shadows, Pat Boone and Gene Vincent. By the 1960s many of the Granada package tours came to Tooting whereby there would be two shows per evening. Acts to play here included The Beatles, The Bee Gees, Roy Orbison, The Troggs, The Honeycombs, The Yardbirds, The Kinks, The Rolling Stones, Little Richard and Gene Pitney. In 1967, there was an eclectic bill featuring The Jimi Hendrix Experience, Engelbert Humperdinck, Cat Stevens and what was to be the last UK performance by the Walker Brothers before they split up. A concert by heavyweight boxing champion turned singer Joe Frazier supported by The New Seekers in 1971 appears to have been the last live music concert held here.

The cinema closed in 1973, to make way for a bingo club. The building has been awarded Grade I listed status by Historic England due to its exceptional architectural importance, a status shared with Buckingham Palace and Tower Bridge.

Granada Woolwich

174-186 Powis Street, Woolwich, SE18 6NL

The Granada opened in 1937 as a cinema with a seating capacity of nearly 2,500 and a lavish interior by Russian-born designer Theodore Komisarjevsky. It was advertised as "The Most Romantic Theatre Ever Built".

Towards the end of the 1950s the Granada Theatre circuit booked live stage acts often with two shows per evening. Many of the most successful acts of the time from both the UK and the USA appeared here between 1958 and 1964. These included The Crickets, Cliff Richard and The Shadows, Eddie Cochran, Billy Fury, Adam Faith, Tommy Steele, Little Richard, The Kinks, The Rolling Stones, The Animals, Chuck Berry, Manfred Mann, The Ronettes and at least five appearances by Gene Vincent. The Beatles played here in 1963 as part of a package tour that also included Roy Orbison and Gerry and the Pacemakers. The latter returned later that year to play another show. Ironically, these days the famous 'Ferry Across the Mersey' that they sang about lays derelict on the River Thames less than a mile away.

In 1966 the cinema was converted into a Granada Social Club and later became a Gala Bingo Club which closed in 2011. The building was bought by a religious organisation in 2011 and is now the Cathedral of Christ Faith Tabernacle and known as the Ebenezer Building.

Lewisham Hippodrome

135-137 Rushey Green, Catford, SE6 2EG

The Lewisham Hippodrome Theatre opened in 1911 as a variety theatre and music hall with an original audience capacity of over 3,000 people though this reduced over time due to internal alterations.

From 1927 it alternated between a cinema and theatre.

Many of the greatest music hall performers of their time performed variety at the Theatre providing comedy, dancing, singing and musical theatre. Some of the entertainers who appeared here included George Robey, Clarice Mayne, George Mozart, Charlie Kunz, Tommy Handley, Laurel and Hardy, Tony Hancock, Max Miller, The Nicholas Brothers and Jessie Mathews. Big bands, operas and circuses also performed here too.

The Hippodrome closed in 1952, ending its days as a live theatre and re-opened as the Eros Cinema later that year. It closed in 1959.

An adjacent cinema, the Gaumont, also closed the same year.

Both were demolished soon after and an office block named Eros House was later built on the site.

THE MAGAZINE PROGRAMME

TWENTY-FOUR PAGES

Lewisham HIPPODROME

The Famous Comedian

GEORGE ROBEY

In a New and Original Entertainment

"HIS SHOW"

Supported by

MARIE BLANCHE

and Full Company

Special Matinees:
THURSDAY and SATURDAY at 2.30
REDUCED PRICES

Iron Curtain Club

231 High Street, Mary Cray, Orpington, BR5 4AX

The basement of this large Georgian house became the Iron Curtain Club from 1965 to 1967.

Live music often took place on Sunday afternoons.

Acts that played here include The Move, The Yardbirds, The Small Faces, The Troggs, The Action, The Moral Set, Geno Washington and the Ram Jam Band, John Mayall and the Bluesbreakers, The Moody Blues, Lee Dorsey and The Who.

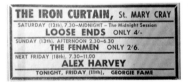

The club was regarded as an iconic Mod venue with DJs specialising in rhythm and blues, soul and ska.

The club's popularity drew lots of attention in this small market town and the authorities closed it down.

The house is now divided into private flats and named Latimer Court.

Mistrale Club

2-4 High Street, Beckenham, BR3 1EW

Situated next door to Beckenham Junction station these premises were formerly the Beckenham Ballroom where The Yardbirds performed in 1964. The Ballroom was renamed the Mistrale Club in 1968, named after the owner's car - a Maserati Mistrale. Manfred Mann played at the grand opening night. One feature of the club was that a vintage Rolls-Royce was used at various times as a DJ booth and as a box office inside the entrance. The venue had three bars spread over two floors.

Many touring acts from the UK and around the world played at the club. These included Bill Haley and His Comets, The Skatalites, Ben E King, The Ethiopians, Ike and Tina Turner, P.P. Arnold, T. Rex, Black Sabbath, Mungo Jerry, Mott the Hoople, The Pyramids, Fleetwood Mac and The Isley Brothers. Some of these acts were at the peak of their careers when they played here. The Nice played here in 1969 after returning from the US before playing at the Lyceum in Central London that same night. Keith Emerson made the Beckenham gig even more memorable by sticking a knife into his keyboard.

The Mistrale also hosted big name BBC Radio One DJs such as Johnnie Walker, John Peel, Kenny Everett and Noel Edmonds. This continued after the live music dried up by late 1971. It became Tites Disco in 1974 when the central ceiling between the ground and first floors was removed to create a single floor warehouse-like club. It later became Lautrec's, then Langtry's, Flux, and is now called The Bridge Bar.

Mistrale Club — Adjoining Beckenham Junction Station — Tel. 01-650 5323

Fri., 28th March

JIGSAW
plus THE CLASSIC.

MISTRALE CLUB
Adjoining Beckenham Junction Station

FORTHCOMING ATTRACTIONS

		Members	Guests
Fri. 4th October	FELICE TAYLOR		
	plus Serendipity	7/6	10/-
Sat. 5th October	GRAND UNION		
	plus The Maddening Crowd	7/6	10/-
Sun. 6th October	Sundae Times	5/-	7/6
Wed. 9th October	Rock Steady Discotheque	2/6	4/-
Thurs. 10th October	Rock Steady Discotheque	4/-	6/-
Fri. 11th October	P.P. ARNOLD		
	plus The Evolution	7/6	10/-
Sat. 12th October	JULIAN KIRSH		
	plus Sweet Rain	7/6	10/-
Sun. 13th October	THE INTER-STATE		
	ROAD SHOW	5/-	7/6
Wed. 16th October	Rock Steady Discotheque	2/6	4/-
Thurs. 17th October	Rock Steady Discotheque	4/-	6/-
Fri. 18th October	TYRANNOSAURUS REX		
	plus PRETTY THINGS		
	also Julian Kirsh	7/6	10/-
Sat. 19th October	HERBIE & THE ROYALISTS		
	plus The Evolution	7/6	10/-
Sun. 20th October	The Skatellites	5/-	7/6
Wed. 23rd October	Rock Steady Discotheque	2/6	4/-
Thurs. 24th October	Rock Steady Discotheque	4/-	6/-
Fri. 25th October	AMBOY DUKES		
	plus Kaleidoscope	7/6	10/-
Sat. 26th October	MR. MO'S MESSENGERS		
	plus Sweet Rain	7/6	10/-
Sun. 27th October	THE PYRAMIDS	5/-	7/6

✳ ✳ ✳ THREE LICENCED BARS 🍸

MISTRALE CLUB LTD.
(adjacent to Beckenham Junction Station)
2 High St., Beckenham (650 5323)

GRAND OPENING
17th APRIL, 1968
MANFRED MANN
and in support The Grenades
Members 10/-, Guests 12/6
18th April, 1968. From the hit parade! "Captain of Our Ship"

REPARATA AND THE DELRONS
— and Popular D.J. DON MOSS
Members 4 - Guests 6
19th April, 1968

DANTALIONS CHARIOT
starring ZOOT MONEY
plus MR. MO'S MESSENGERS
Members 7/6, Guests 10/-
20th April, 1968

PYRAMIDS
and in support The Go-Go Show
Members 7/6, Guests 10/-
24th April, 1968

ALAN PRICE SET
and in support The Grenades
Members 10/-, Guests 12/6
26th April, 1968

MR. MO'S MESSENGERS
Members 5/-, Guests 7 6

SHIRALEE
Members 5/-, Guests 7/6

The Club is comprised of three luxuriously furnished bars, a Discotheque highlighted by a white Vintage Rolls Royce and upstairs you can dance in Romanesque Decor to some of the leading names in the POP, JAZZ, SKA and BLUES WORLD, new members welcome. (All Artistes booked for the Mistrale Club through Star Attractions. RIGwd 8956).

FRIDAY 30TH MAY
THE NICE
PLUS "THE COLOURS"
ADM. 12/6
LICENSED BARS · DISCOTHEQUE
MISTRALE
MEMBERS ONLY · APPLICATIONS 650-5323

MISTRALE CLUB
Adjoining Beckenham Junction Station
Private Members Club
Membership Details from 01-650 5323
APRIL DATES

Thursday 1st	Return to the Swinging 60's	
Friday 2nd	**Jelly Bread**	4/-
Saturday 3rd	**Spencer Mac**	10/-
Sunday 4th	Dave Mitchell's Soul Discotheque	
Wednesday 7th	Dave Mitchell's Soul Discotheque	
Thursday 8th	Rock 'n' Roll with the Housershakers	
Friday 9th	**MOTT THE HOOPLE**	
	Collection	
Saturday 10th	Dave Mitchell's Soul Discotheque	
Sunday 11th	Dave Mitchell's Soul Discotheque	
Wednesday 14th	The Maggi Rock Band	
Thursday 15th		
Friday 16th	**Bonzo Dog Do Da Band**	
	Muma Bear	
Saturday 17th	Dave Mitchell's Soul Discotheque	
Wednesday 21st	Rock 'n' Roll with Jimmy Peck	
Thursday 22nd		
Friday 23rd	**Sam Apple Pie**	10/-
	Hot Jack	
Saturday 24th	Dave Mitchell's Soul Discotheque	
Sunday 25th	Dave Mitchell's Soul Discotheque	
Wednesday 28th	Rock 'n' Roll with Mike L. and the Fire Birds	
Thursday 29th		
Friday 30th	**ASHTON GARDNER & DYKE**	

We would like to remind all members that their membership is due for renewal on May 1st.

DOORS OPEN 8 p.m. · PRICES SHOWN FOR MEMBERS

| OPEN FIVE NIGHTS | WEDNESDAY DISCO | THURSDAY DRINKING SIXTIES | FRIDAY THE ARENA | SATURDAY PARTY NIGHT | SUNDAY SOUL |

MISTRALE CLUB
Adjoining Beckenham Junction Station

Friday, 18th October
THREE STAR BILL

TYRANNOSAURUS REX
The Pretty Things
Julian Kirsch

Members 7/6   Guests 10/-

Wednesday, 25 February	Revolution
Thursday, 26 February	Blaises
Friday, 27 February	Brunel University, Uxbridge
Saturday, 28 February	Essex University, Colchester
Sunday, 1 March	Farx Club, Southall
Monday, 2 March	Mistrale Club, Beckenham
Tuesday, 3 March	Upstairs at Ronnie Scott's

Marcus Bicknell
01-937 3793
No sole agency

GENESIS

MISTRALE CLUB
Adjoining Beckenham Junction Station

FRIDAY 29th NOV
RADIO 1 FAVOURITES
The Kaleidoscope
plus THE MOJOS
Members 7/6
Guests 10/-

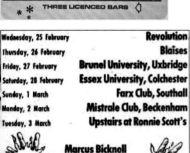

Montague Arms

289 Queen's Road, New Cross, SE15 2PA

This pub was decked out with an eclectic bunch of curios ranging from nautical gear to taxidermy including a stuffed zebra head looking out of an old horse-drawn carriage. The Sun newspaper reviewed the pub describing the decor as "like a pirate ship in The Goonies." There were signs displayed outside proclaiming "Coaches Welcome" which looked a little odd in this neighbourhood. In fact the pub had deals with cross-channel drivers, and coaches full of tourists used to call in for a drink, and sometimes food, while being entertained by house band, The Two Petes, who were a blind keyboard player and a drummer who was also the pub owner. They had been playing there since 1970 and in their early days they released Live at the Montague Arms albums. Comedians Jimmy Jones, Jim Davidson and Mike Reid all began their careers performing at this pub. Pete the owner told customers that Paul McCartney once made an impromptu appearance and played a few songs in the 1980s after Jim Davidson recommended the pub to him when they met on a flight. In addition to The Two Petes the pub hosted club nights and live music including acts such as Gang of Four, Band of Holy Joy and Anna Calvi.

In 1989 the NME interviewed Shane MacGowan of the Pogues, Mark E Smith of the Fall and Nick Cave together in the Montague Arms who after a few drinks got onstage and jammed together with MacGowan on drums, Smith on guitar and Cave on the organ.

In 2008 The Rough Pub Guide: A Celebration of the Great British Boozer said the Montagu Arms was the best pub in Britain.

Following the passing of long-time managers Stan and Bet who were both in their 80s the pub closed in 2011 but reopened in 2014 with new managers who successfully carried on the tradition of the old regime. There was live music again with performers including Gnarwolves, The Smith Street Band, Shit Present, Iron Chic, Oxygen Thief, Doe, King Krule, Lice and The Phobics plus popular events such as the LGBT club night Passionate Necking.

Despite their popularity live events ceased in 2018 after a change in ownership and the Montague Arms was relaunched soon afterwards with American style pub with games and cocktails though this was unsuccessful and closed in 2019. The pub currently lays vacant.

Odeon/Gaumont Theatre

1-5 Loampit Vale, Lewisham, SE13 7FT

The Gaumont Palace was opened as a cinema in 1932 with Bobby Howell and his Band playing on the opening night. The cinema had seating for just over 3,000 people. It was renamed Gaumont Theatre in 1937.
As well as showing films the Gaumont had stage shows and live music. From the late 1950s acts to play here included Miles Davis Quintet, Helen Shapiro, Cliff Richard and The Shadows, Bobby Darin, Duane Eddy, Gene Vincent, and Adam Faith.

One night in 1962, towards the end of a matinee film performance, a fire caused extensive damage. After being repaired the cinema reopened later that year renamed the Odeon and films and concerts were held here for the next 19 years. Big names to have played at the Odeon in the 1960s include Stevie Wonder, The Hollies, Gene Pitney, Joe Cocker, The Rolling Stones and Ray Charles. The Beatles played two dates here in 1963. By the time they played the second time fans camped outside for tickets and before the gig the band were driven to nearby Ladywell Police Station, from where they were given a police escort to the venue. The Odeon continued to put on big names throughout the 1970s including Black Sabbath, Bo Diddley, Canned Heat, T. Rex, Emerson, Lake and Palmer, Van Halen, Status Quo, Thin Lizzy, Bay City Rollers, Dr. Feelgood, Sparks, David Bowie, Faces, David Essex, Deep Purple, Ian Dury and The Blockheads, The Police, Wings, Queen, Siouxsie and The Banshees and The Specials. In 1980, there were concerts by The Clash, Hawkwind, Adam and The Ants and Yes. The Odeon closed down the following year with The Who playing two concerts the week before closure.

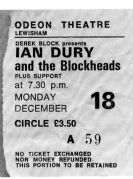

ODEON THEATRE
LEWISHAM
DEREK BLOCK presents
IAN DURY
and the Blockheads
PLUS SUPPORT
at 7.30 p.m.
MONDAY
DECEMBER **18**
CIRCLE £3.50
A 59
NO TICKET EXCHANGED
NOR MONEY REFUNDED
THIS PORTION TO BE RETAINED

The Odeon was left derelict for ten years before the building was demolished in 1991 to allow for a road widening scheme. These days this part of Lewisham is barely recognisable.

GAUMONT, LEWISHAM

SUNDAY, JANUARY 24th 6 & 8.30 p.m.

ED. W. JONES presents

JACK PARNELL ORCHESTRA + TANNER SISTERS
VICTOR SEAFORTH + AUDREY JEANS

3/- to 6/- (LEE 1331)

Outlaw Concerts Present

DIRE STRAITS

LEWISHAM ODEON

Tuesday 18th December
Wednesday 19th December

SOLD OUT

RAINBOW

Thursday 20th December
Friday 21st December

STRAIGHT MUSIC PRESENTS

THE **SPECIALS**
THE **SELECTER**

DEXY'S MIDNIGHT RUNNERS

LEWISHAM ODEON
LOAMPIT VALE S.E.13.

SATURDAY 1st DECEMBER at 7·30

TICKETS £3.00 £2·50 £2·00 (INC.VAT) IN ADVANCE THEATRE BOX OFFICE, 852 1331, LONDON THEATRE
BOOKINGS, SHAFTESBURY AVE., 439 3371. PREMIER BOX OFFICE, 240 2245. USUAL AGENTS OR ON NIGHT

Dave Woods Present

SIOUXSIE
& THE

BANSHEES
with special guests

THE CURE

Saturday 13th October
LEWISHAM ODEON

Doors Open 7 pm

Advance tickets: £3, £2.50 and £2 from Box Office Loampit Vale.
London S.E. 13, Telephone 01-852 1332

Odeon/Coronet

John Wilson Street, Woolwich, SE18 6QQ

The Odeon was designed in an Art Deco style by architect George Coles.

The cinema opened in 1937 with seating for over 1,800 people.

Towards the end of the days of the Odeon, live acts were introduced from 1979. These included Dizzy Gillespie, UB40, Hazel O'Connor and Girlschool. In 1981 Diamond Head played here watched by Lars Ulrich who says that it was this gig that was responsible for inspiring Metallica, the band he formed a few months after the Woolwich gig.

The Odeon closed later on in 1981 and re-opened as the Coronet Cinema in 1983. Live acts to play The Coronet during the 1980s include Level 42, New Order, Hawkwind, Xmal Deutschland, The Fall and local lads Squeeze. Fiendish Shadows by The Damned is a live album of their gig here and the 12 inch version of 'Spirit in the Sky' the number one chart single by Doctor and the Medics features bonus live tracks recorded at the Coronet.

The Coronet closed in 1999 and has been converted into a place of worship by the New Wine Church with the building renamed Gateway House.

193

Orchid Ballroom/Tiffany's

112 Brighton Road, Purley, CR8 4DB

The Orchid Ballroom opened in 1950 replacing Europe's largest ice rink which was previously on the site. The Orchid was listed in the Guinness Book of Records as the largest ballroom in the UK and hosted dances with music provided by resident band leader Johnny Howard and his Orchestra and visiting orchestras such as the Ted Heath Band with his regular singers Lita Roza, Dennis Lotis and Dickie Valentine. In the early 1960s the Orchid played host to BBC TVs Come Dancing, the fore-runner of today's Strictly Come Dancing.

As the big band era began to wane and attendances declined the business was taken over by Mecca in 1962 and the Orchid became a popular venue for up-and-coming bands, as well as for established acts such as Jr. Walker and The All Stars, Percy Sledge, Mary Wells, The Who, Status Quo, Small Faces, The Hollies, The Jimi Hendrix Experience, The Spencer Davis Group and Stevie Wonder. The early 1970s saw performances by Slade, Family, The Sweet and Deep Purple.

In 1973, the Orchid changed its name to Tiffany's and held a popular disco often with glam rock chart acts such as Mud, Wizzard and Suzi Quattro. Later in the 1970s there were gigs by new wave and punk bands such as The Clash, Siouxsie and The Banshees, The Pretenders, The Human League and The Slits. Slade and Queen also played here during this period.

Tiffany's remained a dance club though live music stopped by 1980 apart from the odd live PA by singers with backing tracks. Over the years it was renamed Cinderella Rockerfella's then Jaz and finally Metropol which closed down in 1998 after losing its licence following complaints of anti-social behaviour by clubbers. The venue is now a fitness club.

Savoy Rooms/The Witchdoctor

75 Rushey Green, Catford, SE6 4AF

Before the Second World War this was known as the Savoy Ballroom. In 1939 it was commandeered by the government for social services, providing food, drink and medicine to local schoolchildren. In the 1960s it became the Savoy Rooms with a gaming club called Mr Smiths on the ground floor and dancing and bands upstairs. The Rolling Stones and Gene Vincent played here in 1964.

The live music club was renamed The Witchdoctor in 1965 and presented acts that included Dave Dee, Dozy, Beaky, Mick and Tich, Jimmy Cliff, The Equals, The Who, The Ethiopians, The Creation, The Skatalites and Desmond Dekker plus smaller popular club circuit bands such as The Loose Ends and The Coloured Raisins. Scottish band The Gaylords played here a few times under that name and in their later incarnation as Marmalade.

The owners of Mr Smiths asked South London gangsters Eddie Richardson and Frankie Fraser to protect the club in exchange for gaming machines being placed there. In 1966 a fight broke out in the early hours of the morning and Richard Hart, an associate of the notorious Kray twins, was shot dead near the bottom of the stairs as he was making his getaway. In revenge Ronnie Kray shot and killed George Cornell, a member of the Richardson gang, at the Blind Beggar pub in Whitechapel the following evening.

Gigs continued until 1969. The ground floor was later converted to retail and the first floor became a snooker hall though in recent years it has been used as a Pentecostal church and is now called the Right Now Jesus Centre.

SeOne

41-43 Saint Thomas Street, London Bridge, SE1 3QX

SeOne, situated underneath the railway arches of London Bridge Station opened in 2002 and was billed as London's largest licensed nightclub with a capacity of 3,000.

The club had five different spaces and held a wide variety of club nights including events by fetish club Torture Garden and Moondance raves. As for live music Aphex Twin and Pendulum played here in 2005 and in 2006 The Klaxons, Shit Disco and Metronomy played an all-ages Christmas matinee show. Between 2006 and 2008 the club hosted the popular Insomniacs Ball, an indie-dance crossover afternoon to sunrise party. In addition to DJs each event would have over a dozen bands which included at various time Art Brut, British Sea Power, The Twang, The Pipettes, The Young Knives, Joe Lean and the Jing Jang Jong, Neils Children, Blood Red Shoes, Brakes and We Smoke Fags. Talking of cigarettes, the club had a controversial policy which charged for a wristband to enter the smoking area.

In 2008 a man was shot dead inside the club and the following year a DJ who was performing a set at a Latin-themed event was beaten up outside causing him life altering injuries.

SeOne closed in 2010 after the owners declared that they found it difficult to fill the club other than on Saturday nights. A new club reopened called Debut London but that lasted only a few months. Jamiroquai and Hercules and Love Affair played gigs here during the new club's short life.

The venue was demolished as part of the redevelopment of London Bridge station when the arches were rebuilt. The area where the club was situated now forms part of the new station concourse.

Thames Polytechnic

Calderwood Street, Woolwich, SE18 6HU

This was the second-oldest polytechnic in the United Kingdom having been founded in 1891 as the Woolwich Polytechnic Young Men's Christian Institute. In 1970 Woolwich Polytechnic merged with other higher education institutions to form Thames Polytechnic.

The Student Union hosted events in the main hall which was a 1930s extension to the original building. When still Woolwich Polytechnic in the late 1960s, Caravan, The Kinks and Genesis played shows and in 1968 there was an all-nighter here when Pink Floyd played at 2am to only 50 people. Hawkwind, The

Pretty Things, Gong, UFO, Van der Graaf Generator and Budgie played during the 1970s as well as punk bands such as Buzzcocks, The Adverts, The Stranglers and Penetration. These gigs also attracted local skinheads and a gig by The Lurkers in 1978 was disrupted by British Movement supporters.

By the 1980s most of the live music was held in the Cellar Bar which was noted for its low ceiling and intimate atmosphere. It hosted a wide selection of gigs from anarcho-punk to indie pop bands. These included Conflict, The Wedding Present, Nico, Sonic Youth, The

June Brides, The Pastels, Jesus and Mary Chain, Levellers, Creaming Jesus, Doctor and the Medics, The Mekons, Television Personalities, The Sugarcubes and Alternative TV. Some of the gigs were immortalised on a double live album compilation called Communicate!!!! Live at Thames Poly recorded in 1985.

In 1992 the Polytechnic was granted university status and renamed University of Greenwich. In 2001 the university gave up its main Woolwich site. The building is currently vacant and is earmarked for community use.

Thomas A' Becket

320 Old Kent Road, SE1 5UE

Medieval pilgrims travelling from London to the tomb of Saint Thomas à Becket in Canterbury would have made their first stop close to this spot. More recently, the Thomas a Becket housed a boxing gym on the first floor of this pub, frequented by all the top names in British boxing, among them Henry Cooper. The body-builder Dave Prowse, (probably better known as the original Darth Vader), was photographed here with Muhammed Ali. In the early 1970s David Bowie rehearsed The Rise and Fall of Ziggy Stardust and The Spiders from Mars on the second floor, while James Fox trained in the boxing gym for his part in Performance. Local lore insists that one of the rooms is so heavily haunted that no one can spend more than five minutes in it before fleeing in terror.

The pub was locally well known for hosting live music especially during the 1970s and 1980s with numerous gigs by pub rockers Sprinkler, Blunderbus, The Tumblers, Scarecrow and Hocus Poke. Progressive jazz rock band Fusion Orchestra, whose singer went on to join Shakatak, played here many times in the early 1970s and local lads Nine Below Zero were spotted playing here in 1979 resulting in a record deal with a major label. Into the 1980s there were gigs by mod bands 007 and The Directions (whose members later formed Big Sound Authority), skinhead band Last Resort and New Wave of British Heavy Metal band Marquis de Sade. Punk bands Guitar Gangsters and The Guttersnipes played here in 1990.

The pub has reopened and closed as a restaurant and nightclub many times in recent years often due to alleged criminal activity and licensing issues. The Thomas A Becket is currently a Vietnamese restaurant. The building carries a blue plaque commemorating the link to Sir Henry Cooper.

Note: *Thomas A' Becket* was on the old pub sign still on the building, the more recent blue plaque says *Thomas a Becket*.

THE BECKETT
320 OLD KENT ROAD, SE1

BRIAN BRAIN + Modern Jazz
THE SCENE + The Cheaters
MERTON PARKAS + Modern Jazz
CHRIS HUNT'S CABLE CAR + Holograms

THE BECKETT
320 OLD KENT ROAD, SE1

Thursday 7th August
CHICKEN SHACK + The Zoots
Monday 11th August
THE BLADES + New Cross
Tuesday 12th August
NUTHIN' FANCY + Vendettas
Wednesday 13th August
MARTIAN DANCE + Petite & The Carbon Units

THOMAS A BECKETT
320 OLD KENT ROAD, LONDON, S.E.1

Thurs. 9th   SPEED-O-METERS
Mon. 13th   MONOS
Tues. 14th   SHADOWFAX
Wed. 15th   TIGER ASHBY

THOMAS A BECKETT
320 OLD KENT ROAD, LONDON, S.E.1

16th   TOUR DE FORCE
        ALL GIRL GROUP
20th   TOUR DE FORCE
21st   THE FAMOUS PLAYERS
22nd   THE RUTS

THOMAS A BECKETT
320 OLD KENT ROAD, LONDON, S.E.1

Thurs. 5th   TIGER ASHBY
Mon. 9th   YOUNG BUCKS
Tues. 10th   SISTER LOUISE
Wed. 11th   MONOS

THOMAS A BECKETT
320 OLD KENT ROAD, LONDON, S.E.1

12th: BENNY AND THE JETS
16th: YOUNG BUCKS
17th: ZHAINE
18th: TIGER ASHBY
(ex-BE BOP DELUXE and ex-XRAY SPECS)

GUTTERSNIPES
AT THE
THOMAS A' BECKETT
320 OLD KENT ROAD
LONDON SE.1

GUITAR GANGSTERS
THE COVERS

ELEPHANT & CASTLE TUBE.
BUS: 21, 42, 53, 63, 141, 177.
8pm – 12.30am / Adm. £2–

Bar & Vietnamese Food

203

The Tiger's Head

350 Bromley Road, Southend, Catford, SE6 2RZ

The Tiger's Head public house put on regular gigs during the mid to late 1960s. The pub was a very popular location for the Bonzo Dog Doo-Dah Band who played here over 30 times during their early years. As a tribute to their early gigs, the band recorded a live album at the London Astoria in 2006 playing their

old songs. The album is called Wrestle Poodles...And Win! The Tiger's Head Days and features special guests Stephen Fry, Phill Jupitus, Adrian Edmondson and Paul Merton. Other acts to play here between 1965 and 1968 include John Mayall's Bluesbreakers, Delroy Williams, Marmalade, The Love Affair, Freddie Fingers and The Upper Hand, The Riot Squad, The Shevelles, Downliners Sect, The Gass, Them, Coloured Raisins and Tony Rivers and The Castaways. Tom Jones performed here in 1965 to fulfil a booking made several months beforehand when he was still relatively unknown. By the time the Tiger's Head gig came round he was number one in the charts with 'It's Not Unusual' and of course subsequently played to a packed-out pub.

Bands continued to play at the Tiger's Head with gigs in the 1970s by bands such as The Charlemagnes, Crafty Fags, Yakety Yak and Gentleman's Relish. The pub's last incarnation was as part of the JD Wetherspoon chain but that closed in 2006 and was demolished in 2010 to make way for a housing development called Deslandes Place.

AT THE "TIGER'S HEAD,"
BROMLEY ROAD, CATFORD, 8 p.m.:
South London Jazz Club presents
BOURBON STREET RAMBLERS.

Trocadero Cinema

1 New Kent Road, Elephant & Castle, SE1 6TE

The Trocadero opened in 1930 as a 3,500-capacity cinema and was considered to be one of the finest movie palaces in the world.

As well as films, the Trocadero over its lifetime hosted variety shows, orchestras, opera and even a full circus. Duke Ellington visited England for the first time in 1933 and played a concert here, presented by the music paper Melody Maker.

Frank Sinatra, David Whitfield, Petula Clark and Ray Ellington all performed shows here in the early 1950s. When the film Rock Around the Clock was shown here there were incidents that made headline news after Teddy Boys slashed the seats and turned on fire hoses. Outside the cinema flying bottles injured two policemen and shop windows were smashed. Chas McDevitt Skiffle Group, Paul Anka and The John Barry Seven played in 1957 and Buddy Holly and the Crickets played two shows on one day in 1958 selling a total of 4,500 tickets. Kenny Lynch, Duane Eddy, Bobby Darin, Cliff Richard and The Shadows and The Four Freshmen also played here before the cinema closed in 1963.

The Trocadero Cinema was promptly demolished following closure and an office block called Alexander Fleming House, (now converted to residential and renamed Metro Central Heights), and an Odeon cinema were built on the site, both designed by noted architect Erno Goldfinger.

The original Wurlitzer organ from the Trocadero is currently installed at the Troxy Cinema in east London. Both the Troxy and the Trocadero were designed by celebrated architect George Coles (see also the Gaumont State Cinema in Kilburn and the Coronet in Woolwich)

The Odeon was demolished in 1988 to be replaced by a residential block. A commemorative plaque was unveiled in 2008 by television presenter Denis Norden, who was assistant manager at the Trocadero Cinema during the second World War.

WEST & SOUTH WEST

All Saints Hall

Powis Gardens, Notting Hill, W11 1JE

The Hall was adjacent to the All Saints Church which opened in 1861.

In 1966 the London Free School was set up to offer alternative adult education. They were also among the groups who set up the first Notting Hill Carnival. Pink Floyd manager Peter Jenner was involved with the school and set up fundraisers at the 300-person capacity Hall with formative shows by Pink Floyd becoming a regular fixture. The band played numerous shows here during the latter part of 1966. Jenner later put on a number of free concerts in London's Hyde Park which included the 1969 concert by The Rolling Stones.

In 1969 the Hall held weekly gigs including the first ever show by Group X, before they changed their name to Hawkwind Zoo and then later to just Hawkwind. DJ John Peel was in the audience and the short set that they played earned them a management contract. They played more gigs in the Hall over the next few months. Other acts to perform here that year included Skin Alley, High Tide, Quintessence, the Third Ear Band, David Bowie, The Crazy World of Arthur Brown, Alexis Korner, Edgar Broughton Band and The Action.

The church is still there and functional, but the Hall was demolished in 1972 to make way for new church facilities and housing.

Assembly Rooms

138 Maple Road, Surbiton, KT6 4RT

The Assembly Rooms were constructed in 1889 with various extensions added  to the building over the years. The main hall with a capacity of just a few hundred people screened films from 1910 and from the 1920s it was used for dances and amateur dramatic productions.

The weekly Surbiton and Kingston Folk Club, a popular club not just confined to folk, formed by singer and guitarist Derek Sarjeant was based at the Assembly Rooms from 1962 to the mid 1970s. Sarjeant would perform regularly at the club when he wasn't on tour and other musicians to perform at the club included Jesse Fuller, Paul Simon, Ralph McTell, Sonny Terry, Tom Paxton, Diz Disley, Sandy Denny, John Renbourn, Stéphane Grappelli and Julie Felix. The club was popular with other musicians and over the years Mick Jagger, Eric Clapton and Donovan were spotted in the audience. The 1960s also saw regular jazz nights held at the Assembly Rooms.

In 1970 Black Sabbath and Yes played here and during the mid 1980s local band Cardiacs played here four times, one of which being a support slot to Nick Cave and The Bad Seeds. The Fall also played here in 1984.

ROY HARPER

Thursday 10th December

The Assembly Rooms
Maple Road, Surbiton
Doors Open 7.30pm
£ 7.50 Ticket No. 154 Tel : 081 390 5078

One infamous gig was when Conflict, Icons of Filth and Lost Cherrees played the Anarchist Ball in 1985. The following day nationwide press described the event as a riot after a pitched battle on the streets of Surbiton between gig-goers and a dozen van loads of police.

JAZZ '67
at SURBITON
(ASSEMBLY ROOMS)
TUES., FEB. 28, 8 p.m.
BOB BARTER
ORCHESTRA
Guest: BOB BURNS
Licensed Bar   Admission 4/-

Public use of the hall continued until 1990 before it was sold off by the council. The whole building is now occupied by Surbiton High School.

CONFLICT
Lost Cherrees
ICONS OF FILTH
THE LEGION OF PARASITES
ADMIT YOU'RE SHIT
STIGMA
AT
SURBITON ASSEMBLY ROOMS
MAPLE RD, SURBITON
FRIDAY MAY 8 1981

CONFLICT
ICONS OF FILTH
Lost Cherrees
stigma
LEGION OF PARASITES
A.Y.S.
Surbiton assembly ROOMS
THURSDAY 9 MAY
£1.50 - 7 bands

THE SOUND
cardiacs "departure"
& PURPLE GANG
AT SURBITON ASSEMBLY ROOMS
ON THU JULY 26th

SURBITON ASSEMBLY ROOMS
MAPLE ROAD, SURBITON TEL 01-399-6553

THURSDAY 29TH MARCH 8pm-12

HERE AND NOW £2.50
+ PRIVATE PATIENTS + GUESTS

ADVANCE TICKETS FOR ALL GIGS
FROM: HARD TIMES RECORDS
THE APPLE MARKET, KINGSTON-UPON-THAMES
(TEL 01-546-4324)

ENQUIRIES: 549-8056 } AFTER 6pm
546-3246

Surbiton Assembly Rooms
GINGER'S
• CLUB •
EVERY MONDAY
8—11 p.m.
Opening 2nd April
with
CHARLIE GALBRAITH'S
JAZZMEN
(FREE membership opening night)
3/6

SURBITON ASSEMBLY ROOMS
MAPLE ROAD, SURBITON 01-399 6553

Wednesday 30th May   8pm-12
NICK CAVE and THE BAD SEEDS
(Ex Birthday Party)
+ THE MOODISTS + CARDIACS
£2 unwaged. £3 in adv.
£3.50 on door

Thursday 7th June   8pm-12
THE ENID   £3 adv
+ SUPPORT   £3.50 door

Thursday 14th June   8pm-12
EEK-A-MOUSE   £4.50 adv
+ JAH MALLAH   £5.00 door

BAR TO 11.30. CASH BUFFET
TICKETS: HARD TIMES RECORDS 01-546 4324

213

Blaises Club

121 Queensgate, South Kensington, SW7 5LP

This club was named after the comic strip character Modesty Blaise and was located in the basement of the Imperial Hotel. It was an upmarket club with roulette and blackjack tables and was a popular hangout for people in the music business.

Many popular acts of the day performed at Blaises from the mid-late 1960s such as The Byrds, The Creation, Brian Auger and The Trinity with Julie Driscoll, Gladys Knight and The Pips, José Feliciano, The Sweet, The N'Betweens (later to become Slade), The Pretty Things and Pink Floyd. Yes, who lived around the corner at the time, stepped in to cover a last-minute cancellation by Sly and The Family Stone in 1968 went on to play here numerous times afterwards. One of the most legendary gigs was when Jimi Hendrix appeared here in 1966 in front of a star-packed crowd including Pete Townshend and Jeff Beck. A Melody Maker review of the gig said "Jimi looks like becoming one of the big club names of 67." Blaises can be seen for a few minutes in the 1967 horror film The Sorcerers starring Boris Karloff where Toni Daly with Lee Grant and the Capitols are performing onstage.

The club carried on into the very early 1970s with performances by Genesis, Hawkwind, Heatwave, Stackridge and Thin Lizzy, though by 1973 there was no regular live music at the venue. The Imperial Hotel closed in the late 1980s, was demolished a few years later and since then the vacant land has been used as a makeshift car park.

Blue Moon

Hayes FC, Church Road, Hayes, UB3 2LE

The Blue Moon club started in 1960 and was situated in the clubhouse of Hayes Football Club. The promoters also ran a Blue Moon club in Cheltenham in addition to the New Georgian Club in Cowley, the Fender Club in Kenton as well as helping organise the Uxbridge Blues and Folk Festival held at the Hillingdon Borough Show Ground.

BLUE MOON

Hayes, Middlesex

Sunday, January 24th

JOHN MAYALL

BLUE MOON
Church Road · Hayes

SUN. 20th MARCH

STEAM PACKET

featuring LONG JOHN BALDRY,
ROD STEWART, JULIE DRISCOLL
and BRIAN AUGER TRINITY

SUN. 27th MARCH

CLIFF BENNETT

SUN. 3rd APRIL

JOHN MAYALL
featuring Eric Clapton

The Blue Moon in Hayes was held mainly on Sunday evenings and put on live acts every week. Some names to play here included Cliff Bennett and The Rebel Rousers, Screaming Lord Sutch & The Savages, Downliners Sect, Lee Dorsey, The Yardbirds, Georgie Fame & The Blue Flames, John Mayall's Bluesbreakers, The Spencer Davis Group, The Who, Steampacket and Cream. By 1967 the live acts ceased and the music nights changed into a disco called the A Train.

BLUE MOON
Church Road, Hayes

SUN. 27th JUNE
SPENCER DAVIS

SUN. 4th JULY
RONNIE JONES

SUN. 11th JULY
GEORGIE FAME

SUN. 18th JULY
CHRIS FARLOWE

SUN. 25th JULY
JOHN MAYALL

SUN. 1st AUGUST
RAMJAM BAND
featuring GENO WASHINGTON

The football club, by now called Hayes and Yeading FC, vacated their ground in 2011 and now play at Yeading FC's former home, The Warren currently known as the SkyEx Community Stadium. The Church Road site has been demolished and replaced with a housing development called Holmesgate Place.

Blue Moon

215

The Bottom Line

56 Shepherd's Bush Green, W12 8TT

Originally opened as the Shepherd's Bush Cinematograph Theatre in 1910 by entrepreneur Montagu Pyke as part of his chain of picture houses. The cinema had a number of name changes over the years and finally stopped showing films in 1981, by which time it was known as the Odeon 2. The main Odeon was in a building next door.

After standing empty for several years, in 1993 it was converted into a live music venue called the Bottom Line, which hosted already established acts including Jefferson Starship, The Revillos, Manfred Mann's Earth Band, Snowy White, Canned Heat, Samson, Link Wray, The Quireboys and Paddy Goes to Holyhead. In 1995 Def Leppard played an acoustic show here on the same day as playing in Morocco and Canada setting a World Record by playing three concerts on three different continents in one day to promote their Vault Greatest Hits 1980-1995 album. Also in 1995 Roger Daltrey and John Entwistle performed here with Simon Townshend standing in for older brother Pete at a Who Fan Convention. Heather Myles recorded a live album at the Bottom Line and a DVD was released of an Eddie and the Hot Rods gig. A musical called Too Much Too Young also had a short residency here in 1995.

The Bottom Line was then refitted as an Australasian-themed bar called Walkabout, which closed down in 2013. A condition of the planning permission was that the facade and the side elevation would be retained as it displayed original signage reading "Cinematograph Theatre, Continuous Performances, seats 1/-6d & 3d".

A new tower has been built into the old facade but during demolition the brittle signage broke up, although a replica has replaced it.

THE BOTTOM LINE
Shepherd's Bush Green
4 - 15 April

LONDON BUBBLE

TOO MUCH TOO YOUNG
BY Catherine Johnson

PALLADIUM

Botwell House

Botwell Lane, Hayes, UB3 2AB

This venue was run in a church hall attached to the early-19th-century Botwell House by an American Priest called Father Gamm to raise parochial funds. Dances with live bands were held several nights of the week during the early to mid 1960s under the club moniker of the Peppermint Stick.

Local Hayes band The Javelins played here numerous times and other acts to play included Frankie Reid and The Casuals, The Rolling Stones, The Tridents, Georgie Fame and The Blue Flames, Them and The Who. Father Gamm also organised two Botwell festivals held in 1963 and 1964 on the playing field at the side of the church hall which was used as the changing room for the groups involved. Servicemen from the US base at Ruislip dug BBQ pits to roast an ox to feed the customers with proceeds going to the church. Advertised as "London's Greatest Ever Open Air Pop Festival", these one day events were some of the first 'pop' festivals ever to be held in the UK. Del Shannon, Freddie and The Dreamers, Gerry and The Pacemakers, Brian Poole and The Tremeloes, Kenny Lynch and Billy J. Kramer and The Dakotas were some names to appear at the 1963 festival. The Animals, Migil 5, The Searchers, The Gamblers and Julie Grant all appeared at the 1964 festival. Screaming Lord Sutch and The Savages performed at both festivals. At one appearance Sutch arrived onstage having leapt out of a coffin with a huge axe, which he then used to chase the audience.

Botwell House is still owned by the Church but has not hosted gigs since 1965.

The Bull

262 Upper Richmond Road West, East Sheen, SW14 7JE

An inn was originally built here in 1792 then rebuilt in 1939 on the same site. An upstairs room hosted many credible acts between 1969 and 1972 including Strawbs, Zoot Money Music Band with Mike Cotton, Caravan, Uriah Heep, Arthur Conley, The Upsetters, Georgie Fame, Prince Buster, Max Romeo, Chicken Shack, Fleetwood Mac, The Equals and Johnny Otis. During

1973 popular Radio 1 DJ John Peel played sounds every Sunday evening. There was a resurgence in live music at The Bull in the mid 1980s with gigs by Flesh for Lulu, The Cherry Bombz, Twenty Flight Rockers, The Membranes, Suspect, Cannes and The Godfathers before the pub closed down.

The Bull was demolished in 1987 to be replaced by shops.

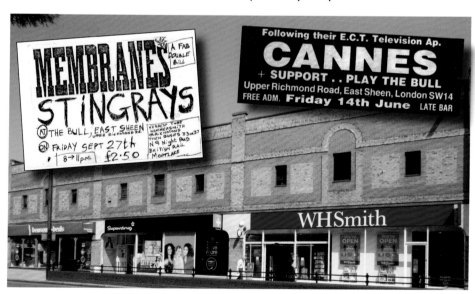

Burton's/Acid Palace

55b Windsor Street, Uxbridge, UB8 1JZ

Montague Burton valued the temperance movement's campaign against the consumption of alcohol and aimed to provide local alternatives to public houses. He installed billiards/snooker halls on the top floors of his Burton menswear stores. This hall, located above the 1930s shop was also the place to dance in the 1950s where bandleaders such as Ted Heath and Joe Loss would bring their orchestras and from the mid 1960s Burton's was the best place in Uxbridge to see charts acts and the finest in up-and-coming live music.

Local band The Birds with their guitarist Ronnie Wood played here regularly during the 1960s and for the rest of the decade the venue hosted gigs several nights a week including shows by The Yardbirds, The Who, Marmalade, Cliff Bennett and The Rebel Rousers, The Skatalites, Amboy Jukes, Jimmy Cliff, Desmond Dekker, Geno Washington and the Ram Jam Band and Coloured Raisins. Being a temperance hall only soft drinks were served at the bar so gig-goers were known to nip out to the adjacent Queens Head pub in the interval between bands.

The club became the Acid Palace in 1969 where Strawbs, Uriah Heep, Genesis, Atomic Rooster, Wishbone Ash, Audience, Lindisfarne, The Groundhogs all played before its demise around 1971.

The building was later demolished to make way for a new shopping precinct currently called The Pavilions. A Pret a Manger coffee shop occupies the exact spot of Burton's. The Queens Head survived and is still going strong.

The Castle

38 Tooting High Street, Tooting, SW17 0RG

The Castle dates from 1832 and is still going strong as a pub though it no longer has live music.

US actor John Wayne reopened the pub in 1948 after a refurbishment, and he was known to pop in for a drink in the early 1950s when in London. Scenes for the 1969 film All Neat in Black Stockings starring Susan George were shot here as were scenes for Citizen Smith in the late 1970s, a popular television sitcom about the self-proclaimed leader of the revolutionary Tooting Popular Front. The Castle has hosted live music since at least the 1940s. John Mayall And The Bluesbreakers played twice in 1966 though the best decade for acts that

went onto further success was the 1970s. Local rhythm and blues band The Marauders fronted by local hairdresser Charlie Harper played here regularly in the 1970s before Charlie went on to form the UK Subs who also played here several times during 1977. Status Quo played here in 1970 supporting Mott The Hoople. The Quo's Rick Parfitt commented that it was a low stage and the audience were all sitting on the floor with their legs apart with their heads down nodding away, so the band decided to copy the audience only looking up between numbers which became a regular on stage pose for the band.

Other acts to play here during the 1970s included Arthur Brown (in Kingdom Come), Argent, Stray, Chicken Shack, Barclay James Harvest, Uriah Heep, The Bee Gees, Blodwyn Pig and The Groundhogs. From the early 1980s mod bands Purple Hearts and The Merton Parkas played here as did many other smaller bands until around 2011 with only The Darkness, who played here in 2001, going on to enjoy greater fame.

These days a marquee has been set up in the pub garden hosting baking competitions as some sort of Tooting's answer to the Great British Bake Off.

The Castle

223

The Cellar Club

22a High Street, Kingston, KT1 1HL

This club started in 1962 in the cellar of a house at 27 Ashdown Road as The Jazz Cellar hosting local Surrey rhythm and blues-based rock and roll acts such as The Nashville Teens, The Stormsville Shakers and Eric Clapton's first band The Roosters plus other bands on the live circuit including Johnny Kidd and The Pirates and The Rolling Stones. Due to its popularity the club moved in 1964 to a former boathouse on the River Thames accessed via a lane to the side of the Odeon Cinema on the High Street.

The new club was renamed the Cellar Club by which time Clapton had joined The Yardbirds. They played at the Club at least ten times during 1964. A gig list

flyer for 20th July that year announces "bird fancier's nite! ... those rare birds from the yard are here...the Yardbirds". Advertisements placed in the music press proclaimed the venue as "The world famous Cellar Club" and listed shows by The Artwoods, The Shondells, Jimmy Winston and The Rebels, The Marvels and Small Faces.

Eric Clapton returned twice in 1965 playing with John Mayall's Bluesbreakers

and in 1966 with his new band Cream who played one of the club's final gigs before it closed down and became a bingo hall.

The building was later demolished, and the site of the club is now luxury residential apartments.

The club's original site was also demolished and is now an open-air car park.

THE CELLAR CLUB

GH STREET, KINGSTON 5856

THIS IS THE NIGHT YOU'VE BEEN WAITING FOR

THE FANTASTIC
KING OF ROCK 'N' ROLL
JERRY LEE LEWIS

ORIGINAL CHECKMATE NASHVILLE TEEN PACKAGE SHOW
LIMITED NUMBER OF TICKETS AT THE DOOR

FRIDAY 27th — A RAVY, SCREAMING GROUP WITH

PHIL & THE STORMVILLE SHAKERS

SATURDAY 28th — BLUE BEAT NIGHT WITH

MICKY FINN & THE BLUESMEN

SUNDAY 29th — BACK BECAUSE THEY'RE SO GOOD

THE ZEPHYRS

OPEN EASTER MONDAY WITH

THE YARDBIRDS

— SORRY, CLOSED

THE CELLAR CLUB
22a HIGH STREET, KINGSTON 5856

WEDNESDAY 1st — FOOLS DAY
THE ANIMALS ARE BACK
SCREAMING R & B
ALSO — THE ORIGINALS

THURSDAY 2nd — GETTING OVER WEDNESDAY

FRIDAY 3rd — A RAVE NIGHT WITH
THE PRESIDENTS

SATURDAY 4th — R & B & ROCK 'n' ROLL WITH
THE BLACK JAYS

SUNDAY 5th — THEY'RE BACK AGAIN
THE SENSATIONAL & EXCITING
DRUIDS

MONADY 6th — R & B WITH THE
YARDBIRDS

TUESDAY 7th — SORRY, CLOSED

Coronation Hall

Denmark Road, Kingston, KT1 2TB

The Coronation Hall was part of the Coronation Baths where one of the swimming pools was boarded over in all but the summer months to form a dance hall and venue for live bands. They were built in the 1930s and named for the coronation of George VI. These days this venue is often confused with the nearby Coronation Hall in Surbiton which is currently a pub. The swimming pool was used during the Second World War for training frogmen underwater for prolonged periods, fixing objects to wooden structures representing enemy coastal defences, and practising cutting submarine nets in preparation for D-Day.

The Hall held jazz and big band dances, one of which was a special New Year's Eve 1964 ball with Ted Heath. During the early 1960s the Hall also hosted blues, pop, soul and rock and roll. Acts included Jimmy Powell and The Five Dimensions, The Zombies, Zoot Money's Big Roll Band, The Tornados, Lulu and The Luvvers, The Yardbirds, P.P. Arnold and The Move. When Gene Vincent played a show here in 1964 he was served with a tax demand by the Inland Revenue claiming unpaid tax for when he was resident in the UK.

The early 1970s saw performances by Fusion Orchestra, Wizzard, Pink Fairies, Caravan and UFO. Later in the decade there were gigs by Siouxsie and the Banshees and local band Cardiac Arrest who later became known as Cardiacs. Sham 69 played a memorable evening in 1978 amid a frenzy of Nazi salutes by a crowd of skinheads one of whom the bouncers threw through the entrance-hall's glass doors while the entire hall turned into a mass brawl, which spilled out into Kingston town centre. The band played for only ten minutes before leaping offstage and making a hasty exit.

The Baths closed in 1979 due to the poor state of the building. It was subsequently demolished.

A residential development aptly named Watersplash Close is now on the site.

Cue Club

5A Praed Street, Paddington, W2 1NJ

The 700 capacity Cue Club in a basement of a small cinema was started up in the mid 1960s by Jamaican born Count Suckle who was previously resident DJ at the Roaring Twenties club in Carnaby Street. The club's name was a reference to its former use as a snooker and billiard hall.

The club played the latest US and Jamaican soul, funk, reggae and ska records as well as featuring live acts such as Stevie Wonder, The Spellbinders Percy Sledge, The Ethiopians, Joe Tex, Mary Wells, The Ronettes, Arthur Conley and Max Romeo. The presence of regular visitors such as Marvin Gaye, Little Richard, Bob Marley, Muhammad Ali and the Commodores gave the place added prestige. Suckle also set up the short-lived Q Records label, a subsidiary of Trojan Records.

The club changed its name to the Q Club and continued on through the 1970s with bands such as Hi-Tension and Misty in Roots playing. The Real Thing made a cameo appearance playing a gig in the 1977 movie Black Joy. The building next door to the club during this period was a social security office where Mick Jones (later of The Clash) worked as a clerical assistant from 1972. The line in the song 'Career Opportunities' about refusing to open letter bombs is a reference to his former job checking mail to make sure they weren't rigged with IRA bombs.

In 1981, the club changed its name again, this time to the People's Club. Tim Westwood DJ'ed a hip-hop night every week when stars like Run-D.M.C., Beastie Boys and Whodini would attend and freestyle into the early hours. Perhaps slightly out of place, Sigue Sigue Sputnik, supported by The Transsexual SS, performed a low-key pre-tour warm up gig here in 1985 when the headline band described the place as dirty and dingy. The club finally closed in 1986 when Suckle retired. The cinema on the ground floor, which by then was showing porn films, closed down at the same time and was demolished in 1989 to be replaced by an office block with an underground car park.

CUE CLUB

THE BEST CLUB IN LONDON
FOR ENTERTAINMENT

5A PRAED STREET, PADDINGTON, W.2
TEL. PAD 5274

Tuesday
DISCOTHEQUE WITH FUNKY RECORDS
LADIES' FREE NIGHT

Wednesday
DISCOTHEQUE WITH FUNKY RECORDS

Thursday
DISCOTHEQUE WITH FUNKY RECORDS
LADIES' FREE NIGHT

day
HE CIMARONS BAND

urday
rom America, the Fabulous
EDDIE FLOYD

day
m America, the Fantastic
TROIT EMERALDS
COUNT SUCKLE SOUND SYSTEM
cords from U.S.A. and JA.
LADIES' FREE NIGHT

ub open 6 nights a week
ase apply for membership
Licensed Bar

Count Suckle Cue Club
5a PRAED STREET, PADDINGTON, W.2
(under The Classic Cinema)

Proudly presents

FRIDAY 3rd February
ON STAGE LIVE
The Fabulous & Fantastic Recording Star
EDWIN STARR
FROM AMERICA

FRIDAY 10th FEBRUARY
Miss MAXIME BROWN
The Fabulous Recording Star from America
ON STAGE LIVE

COUNT SUCKLE Sound System
Latest records from U.S.A. and Ja.

NEXT COMING ATTRACTIONS
17th February ...GARNET MIMMS   24th February ...BARBARA LYNN

★ LADIES FREE NIGHTS THIS YEAR EVERY MONDAY & WEDNESDAY

Club opens seven nights a week. Sunday 7 p.m - 5 a.m.
Monday to Thursday 5.30 p.m. - 4 a.m.   Licensed B
also Restaurant Open the whole night ★This Club is for members o
Members of this Club must be at least 18 years of age.

The Management approve of the smartness of the ladies who come to
the Club.   THE CUE CLUB IS THE LADIES'

★ Join the QUEUE at the CUE CLUB

Please apply for membership from COUNT S
5a PRAED STREET, PADDINGTON, W.2   or   Telephone
Nearest Stations Paddington, Edgware Road   Buses

The Bell Press 396 Portobello Road, W.10 LAD 0881

COUNT SUCKLE'S
CUE CLUB
5A PRAED STREET, W.2
TEL. PAD 5274

Monday - Thursday
COUNT SUCKLE

Friday, April 29th, 6 p.m. 5 a.m.
BLUE RIVERS
AND THE
MAROONS
COUNT SUCKLE

Saturday, April 30th, 6 p.m. 5 a.m.
ALVIN ROBINSON
AND THE
DIXIE CUPS
COUNT SUCKLE

CUE CLUB
5a PRAED STREET, PADDINGTON, W.2
TEL. PAD 5274

COUNT SUCKLE SOUND SYSTEM
with BAND
Latest records from U.S.A. & J.A.

Friday, November 1st
FROM AMERICA
OSCAR TONEY JUNIOR

Saturday, November 2nd
FROM AMERICA
MISS DEE DEE WARWICK

CUE CLUB
THE BEST CLUB IN LONDON
FOR ENTERTAINMENT
5A PRAED STREET, PADDINGTON, W.2
TEL. PAD 5274

Tuesday
DISCOTHEQUE WITH FUNKY RECORDS
LADIES' FREE NIGHT

Wednesday
DISCOTHEQUE WITH FUNKY RECORDS
LADIES' FREE NIGHT

Thursday
DISCOTHEQUE WITH FUNKY RECORDS

Friday
MARVELS BAND

Saturday
PSYCHO & HIS BAND

Sunday
LADIES' FREE NIGHT
DISCOTHEQUE WITH FUNKY RECORDS

Club open 6 nights a week
Please apply for membership
Licensed Bar

Cue Club

Earls Court Exhibition Centre

Warwick Road, SW5 9TA

Earls Court Exhibition Centre was a major exhibition and events venue that opened in 1937 on the site of a former showground. It was used as one of the venues for both the 1948 and 2012 Olympic Games as well as the British International Motor Show, London Boat Show, the Ideal Home Show, Crufts dog show and the Royal Tournament military tattoo among many other high-profile events.

The venue was also one of the largest concert arenas in the UK, with a capacity of around 19,000 and during the 1970s hosted concerts by Slade, David Bowie, Led Zeppelin, Elton John, Pink Floyd, Queen, The Rolling Stones and Bob Dylan.

Pink Floyd returned in 1994 for a 14-night residency but on the first night during their opening song a section of seating collapsed, injuring 90 people. That night's performance was abandoned and re-scheduled for a later date. A tragedy occurred after a four night run by the Spice Girls in 1999 when a worker died after falling 80 feet while dismantling the stage. Other performers to have played here include Oasis, Morrissey, Madonna, Iron Maiden, REM, U2, Kasabian Taylor Swift, Arctic Monkeys, Red Hot Chili Peppers, Westlife, Neil Diamond, Take That and Ariana Grande. Michael Jackson performed at the Brit Awards show here in 1996 when his stage was famously invaded by Pulp's Jarvis Cocker.

With falling attendances and fewer events partly due to the opening of the O2 Arena in 2007, the Earls Court Exhibition Centre closed in 2014 with Bombay Bicycle Club performing the last show with guest Dave Gilmour of Pink Floyd appearing to perform Floyd's 'Wish You Were Here' in a tribute to the venue. Demolition work commenced immediately afterwards. The land is earmarked for property development, but that has yet to materialise. The site is currently vacant.

Gaumont Theatre/The Pavilion

58 Shepherd's Bush Green, W12 8QE

Opened in 1923 as the Pavilion Cinema which had a lavish interior with over 2,000 seats. The films were accompanied by the Pavilion Symphony Orchestra, and a lighting system which created colour effects.

The Pavilion Cinema was taken over by Gaumont British Theatres in 1923. It closed for 11 years after wartime damage and reopened as the Gaumont Theatre in 1955 after a complete rebuilding of the interior. The Gaumont hosted a handful of concerts later that decade including Cliff Richard and The Drifters in 1958 and the following year a bill of Duffy Power, Vince Eager, Vince Taylor and The Playboys and Marty Wilde which according to the media at the time brought hysterical scenes by teenage girls both inside and outside the theatre.

Later it became the Odeon and reconstruction saw the interior split into a

smaller cinema and bingo club. The Odeon closed in 1983 with bingo continuing until 2001. After a period of dereliction part of the building re-opened as The Pavilion, a 700-capacity special event venue which hosted occasional gigs including Ade Edmondson and the Bad Shepherds, Ani DiFranco, Queens of the Stone Age, an All Saints reunion gig and a private gig by Jamiroquai in front of competition winners to celebrate the launch of a mobile phone. The Rolling Stones held an aftershow party here in 2003 after their gig at Wembley Arena.

The Pavilion operated until 2011 and the building was subsequently demolished whilst retaining the building's Grade II listed facade. It is now the 317-bedroom luxury Dorsett Hotel.

Ginglik

1 Shepherd's Bush Green, Shepherds Bush, W12 8PH

This venue was unique in that it was in a converted underground Edwardian public toilet. The 250-capacity venue opened in 2002. The building had also been a snooker club for a while beforehand and held a diverse selection of events including live bands, DJs, exhibitions, cabaret, comedy and martial arts classes.

Live acts to appear at Ginglik on their way to greater success include Ellie Goulding, Paloma Faith, Paolo Nutini and Laura Marling plus others including The Duke Spirit, The Kut, The Soft Pack and The Veils. Dee C Lee, once a member of Central Line and The Style Council and a backing singer for Wham! played a comeback gig in 2009 in her new band Favoured Nations which also included members of Level 42. Acts such as Fay Hallam, The Bongolian, DC Fontana and Bermondsey Joyriders played when the popular club Blow Up had a monthly residency here during 2011 and 2012.

Robin Williams did a surprise gig here as a warm-up for his appearance at the Royal Variety Performance at the London Palladium. Michael McIntyre, Jimmy Carr, Lenny Henry, Frank Skinner and Adam Hills are some of the others who appeared here on the Laugh comedy nights in what The Sunday Times described as "one of London's coolest bars."

Ginglik closed down in 2013 and the venue is currently derelict. Ginglik's Laugh comedy club has relocated to 100 Wardour Street in Soho.

Granada Brixton

10 Brighton Terrace, Brixton, SW9 8DG

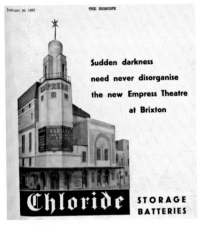

Opened in 1898 as the Empress Theatre, a musical variety hall with seating for over 1,800 people. In 1909 The Bioscope newspaper described the Empress as "one of the finest of London's suburban music halls". The theatre was then re-constructed in an Art Deco style in 1931 and renamed the New Empress Theatre. The theatre hosted many stars including Marie Lloyd, Charlie Chaplin, Harry Lauder, Tony Hancock, Joe Brown, Max Miller, Stan Laurel and Oliver Hardy, and Bruce Forsyth. The New Empress closed as a live theatre in 1957 with Max Miller performing at the last music hall bill before the place reopened as a Granada cinema a year later.

In addition to films the Granada held wrestling matches and pantomimes, plus the occasional live concert. During 1964 there was a one-night special featuring two performances each by Billy J. Kramer and The Dakotas, The Kinks, The Yardbirds and The Ronettes. James Brown and the Famous Flames performed here in 1966. In 1967 the cinema became a bingo club then a furniture store before the building was demolished in 1992. Flats named Pavilion Mansions have since been built on the site.

GRANADA
BRIXTON   BRI. 2201
ON STAGE MONDAY MARCH 2 FOR TWO WEEKS
DON ROSS SAYS "THANKS FOR THE MEMORY"
March 2 week Mon.-Thurs. 7.30. Fri. & Saturday 6.20 & 8.45
HETTY KING • SANDY POWELL
CAVAN O'CONNOR • BILLY DANVERS
                       • MARIE LLOYD
Book Now 4/6 8/6 8/8. Upper Circle (unreserved) 2/6
Call, write or phone REDpost 2600. Box Office open 10.30-8 o/c.
Change of cast March 9 week.   BOOK NOW.

GRANADA BRIXTON phone: RED 2600
STAGE. ONE NIGHT ONLY. SUN 13 MAR. 6o'c & 8.30
FROM AMERICA - MR DYNAMITE
JAMES BROWN
and the FAMOUS FLAMES
AND ALSO FROM AMERICA
BARBARA LEWIS
MIKE COTTON SOUND   MARIONETTES
BRITAIN'S ACE COMPERE - DIRECT FROM BBC'S POP 826
KEITH FORDYCE
7/6 8/6 10/- 12/6 17/6

GRANADA - BRIXTON
Stage — One Show Only
SUNDAY, MARCH 22nd, at 7.30
Joe Collins presents a
HOOTENANNY NIGHT
with
ROBIN HALL & JIMMY MacGREGOR
THE COUNTRYMEN • WALLY WHYTON
STEVE BENBOW • ALEX CAMPBELL
LONG JOHN BALDRY AND THE HOOCHIE COOCHIE MEN
ROD STEWART • LISA TURNER
REDD SULLIVAN • CUMBERLAND 3
MALCOLM PRICE TRIO
BOOK NOW: 5/-, 7/6, 10/6. Phone: RED 2600

GRANADA
BRIXTON   REDpost 2600
ON STAGE SUN. MAR 22   One show only, 7.30
A HOOTENANNY NIGHT
AN EVENING OF FOLK MUSIC
ROBIN HALL   JIMMY McGREGOR
THE COUNTRYMEN   WALLY WHYTON
LONG JOHN BALDRY : THE HOOCHIE COOCHIE MEN
BOOK NOW 5/- 7/6 10/6.   RED. 2600

-A-
V.T.C. THEATRE **EMPRESS**
BRIXTON
BOX OFFICE OPEN FROM 10 A.M.
TELEPHONE BRI 2201.
Chairman: REGINALD C. BROMHEAD   Managing Director: GERARD KEATH   Manager: DOYLE CROSSLEY
6.30 ★ MONDAY, AUGUST 15th, 1955 ★ 8.45
TWICE NIGHTLY
BIG STAR VARIETY BILL
★ STARRING THE ★
FAREWELL ENGAGEMENT OF
DOROTHY SQUIRES
★ STAR OF POLYGON RECORDS ★
PRIOR TO AMERICAN TOUR

GRANADA BRIXTON
JAN 13 to 25 Eves 7.30 Mats Weds Thurs Sats 2.30
JOE BROWN
and the BRUVVERS
IN THE
SPECTACULAR STAGE PANTOMIME
ALADDIN
FULL WEST END COMPANY
BOOK NOW 3/6 4/6 6/6 8/6 phone: RED 2600

GRANADA
ON STAGE JANUARY 13 FOR TWO WEEKS BRIXTON
RING US ON OUR SPECIAL DIRECT LINE
FOR THE BEST SEATS NOW   RED 2600
JOE BROWN **AND THE BRUVVERS**
IN THE SPECTACULAR PANTOMIME
ALADDIN
STALLS 8/6 6/6 4/6 CIRCLE 8/6 6/6 UPPER CIRCLE 4/6 3/6
Special Rates for Parties.

Granada Greenford

229 Greenford Road, Greenford, UB6 8QY

The 2,000 seat Granada Cinema was officially opened in 1937 by the actress and singer Gracie Fields, who had been starring in a film that was being shot at the nearby Denham Studios.

As with many other Granada Cinemas around the UK this one was also used as a concert and wrestling venue. Between 1960 and 1965 the venue hosted many

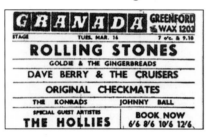

package tours often with two shows per evening. Acts to play included Billy J Kramer, Johnny Kidd and The Pirates, Joe Brown and His Bruvvers, Heinz, Adam Faith, The John Barry Seven, Tommy Steele and numerous appearances by Gene Vincent. The Rolling Stones played here in 1964 and again in 1965. Part of their Got Live If You Want It! EP was recorded here. They were playing as part of a package tour with The Hollies, The Konrads (minus sax player David Jones aka David Bowie who had already left the band) and Dave Berry and The Cruisers.

The Cinema closed in 1966 and soon afterwards it was converted into a branch of Tesco supermarket. Internally there are no obvious clues as to the building's previous use, though parts of the ornate ceiling of the former auditorium are hidden behind a false supermarket ceiling.

There are plans for the whole building to be demolished and replaced by a new supermarket.

THE **ROLLING STONES**

DAVE BERRY AND THE CRUISERS

| THE KONRADS | THE CHECKMATES | Compère JOHNNY BALL |

GOLDIE and the Gingerbreads

GUEST STARS **THE HOLLIES**

TWICE NIGHTLY

EDMONTON REGAL	MAR. 5th	LEICESTER TROC	MAR. 12th
LIVERPOOL EMPIRE	MAR. 6th	RUGBY GRANADA	MAR. 13th
MANCHESTER PALACE	MAR. 7th	ROCHESTER ODEON	MAR. 14th
SCARBOROUGH		GUILDFORD ODEON	MAR. 15th
FUTURIST	MAR. 8th	GREENFORD	
SUNDERLAND ODEON	MAR. 9th	GRANADA	MAR. 16th
HUDDERSFIELD ABC	MAR. 10th	SOUTHEND ODEON	MAR. 17th
SHEFFIELD CITY HALL	MAR. 11th	ROMFORD ABC	MAR. 18th

Granada Greenford

237

Granada Harrow

Manor Parade, Sheepcote Road, Harrow, HA1 2JN

Opened as a cinema in 1937 by local singer and actress Jessie Matthews and with a performance by the Band of the Royal Scots Guard. The interior was by noted interior designer Theodore Komisarjevsky (see also Granada Woolwich and Granada Tooting).

In common with other Granada Theatres, in addition to films the 1,900 seat Harrow venue was used for the staging of rock 'n' roll shows for a few years from 1959 to 1965. A majority of these were package tours, with several well-known groups on the same bill touring the country such as the Group Scene 64 tour which featured The Rolling Stones, The Ronettes, Dave Berry and The Cruisers, Marty Wilde and The Wildcats, Swinging Blue Jeans and The Cheynes. Other acts to play at this Granada include Cliff Richard and The Shadows, Manfred Mann, The Walker Brothers, Roy Orbison, Cilla Black, The Hollies, Little Richard, Joe Brown and The Bruvvers, The Searchers, Little Eva, Dion, Del Shannon, Duane Eddy and Dave Clark Five. PJ Proby was billed to perform in 1965 but after his pant-splitting incident at Croydon he was removed from the bill and replaced at short notice by the lesser-known Tom Jones whose first single, 'It's Not Unusual', had entered the charts at number 39 the previous week.

The cinema closed in 1996 and following a period of dereliction the building now houses a gym. The building has been awarded Grade II listed status by Historic England. As part of the conditions of planning permission the cinema's Wurlitzer organ remains in place on the stage.

Granada Harrow

239

Grosvenor Arms

17 Sidney Road, Stockwell, SW9 0TP

This Victorian backstreet pub began hosting regular live music in 2006 and was popular for its folk sessions in the bar and bands in a function room at the back of the pub.

The Grosvenor was particularly famed for its punk gigs and a mixture of smaller and established names on the circuit played here. These included The Restarts, Menace, Red Flag 77, Splodgenessabounds, The Vibrators, Wonk Unit, Steve Ignorant's Slice of Life, English Dogs, Vice Squad, 16 Guns, Citizen Fish, The Griswalds, Eastfield and Wat Tyler. Other acts included Daevid Allen, The Brixton 49ers, Barking Bateria and The Fallen Leaves.

The pub closed down in 2014 when Severed Limb and The Mountain of Love played the final gig. The pub had been purchased by developers who gutted the pub interior and turned the function room and upper floors into flats. Against all odds the pub reopened in 2019 and is popular with craft beer fans. There will no longer be live music at the pub partly due to the absence of the function room and any bands playing in the bar would likely cause noise disturbance to the new flats.

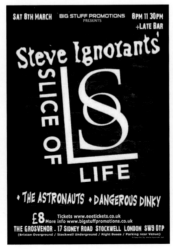

241

Hammersmith Palais

242 Shepherd's Bush Road, W6 7NL

This venue was originally used as a tram depot, then a roller-skating rink before opening as a dancehall in 1919 as Hammersmith Palais De Danse.

Soon after opening, resident acts playing here were the Original Dixieland Jazz Band and the Jazz Kings though by 1929 the worn floor of the venue was transformed into an ice rink. In 1934, the venue was once again converted into a dance hall which carried on into the Second World War and was popular with servicemen on leave. Glenn Miller was among the performers here during this period and the BBC broadcasted a show called Services Spotlight live from the venue. Jazz bands continued after the war and by 1959 Joe Loss was the resident bandleader at the Palais, a role he'd keep for the next decade.

From the 1970s the Palais became a 2,500 capacity (later reduced to 1,500) venue for rock bands such as The Who, The Sweet and Can and later on that decade punk and new wave acts brought more regular gigs including appearances by X-Ray Spex, Elvis Costello and The Attractions, Talking Heads and The Human League. In 1979 The Police played two Hammersmith shows in one night. They travelled the short distance in an armoured military vehicle from their show at the Odeon to another at the Palais. The 1978 Clash song '(White Man) In Hammersmith Palais' was inspired by singer Joe Strummer attending a reggae gig at the venue.

The popularity of the venue increased into the 1980s with Girlschool, Gang of Four, The Jam, The B-52's, U2, Echo and The Bunnymen, Ramones, Iggy Pop, The Clash, The Smiths Bauhaus, Eurythmics, and The Psychedelic Furs among the acts playing gigs here during that decade. During the 1990s Suede, Supergrass, Ocean Colour Scene, Oasis, Massive Attack, Pop Will Eat Itself, Robbie

Williams, The Lightning Seeds, Bush, The Wildhearts, Jet and Basement Jaxx all graced the stage. Gigs dried up in the early 2000s when the venue was sold and renamed Po Na Na which concentrated on club nights although Jay-Z did perform here in 2001 when it was reported that a hostile crowd of several hundred people without tickets attempted to storm the venue.

Another new owner brought back the Hammersmith Palais name and gigs recommenced though a few years later the Palais was condemned for demolition.

The Good, the Bad and the Queen, composed of members of Blur, The Clash and The Verve, played on what was promoted as the Palais' last night. However, The Fall played the following night and the concert was subsequently released as the live album Last Night at The Palais. Though in fact the final gig at the Hammersmith Palais took place a month later in May 2007 with Groove Armada being the last to play there.

The building was finally demolished a few years later and student flats and a gym have been constructed on the site. An old hand-painted advertising sign for the Hammersmith Palais de Danse on its surviving rear boundary wall is still visible from the platform of Hammersmith station.

Hammersmith Palais

243

Hanging Lamp

The Crypt, St Elizabeth of Portugal Church, The Vineyard, Richmond, TW10 6AQ

The Hanging Lamp was an intimate folk club formed in 1968 in the crypt of a church constructed in 1824 just off Richmond Hill.

The club with capacity for around 150 people who sat on wooden benches and the floor or stood at the back against the vaulted brick walls featured popular singers on the folk circuit including John Martyn who played here every few months over the next four years. One of his performances at the club was later released as an album. Other performers included Frank McConnell, Strawbs, Ralph McTell, Gordon Giltrap, Tír na nÓg, Pete Atkin, Al Stewart and Elton John's future guitar player Davey Johnstone. Elvis Costello recalls in his autobiography that he gave his first public performance here, then called Declan MacManus, when he was only 14 years old. He spotted folk legend Ewan MacColl asleep during his performance. A young brother and sister duo called The Sallyangie duo played the Hanging Lamp regularly. The brother, Mike Oldfield, later went onto worldwide solo success.

The Hanging Lamp club closed in 1972. In recent years the crypt has been renovated and converted into a church hall. Still on a musical theme, the church itself hosted the wedding of Thin Lizzy's Phil Lynott in 1980 and his funeral in 1986. Barbara Dickson also got married here in 1984.

244

Hobbit's Garden/William Morris Club

267 The Broadway, Wimbledon, SW19 1SD

This club was situated in William Morris House, a Labour Club and community space named after the Victorian textile designer, artist and socialist who had a workshop nearby.

From late 1970 the William Morris House hosted Hobbit's Garden, a short-lived hip club, who put on gigs there by Hawkwind, Status Quo, Strawbs, Caravan, Thunderclap Newman, Stray, Vinegar Joe, Roxy Music and Genesis.

Between 1987 and 1989 the venue hosted many hardcore and punk nights with Bolt Thrower, Napalm Death, The Instigators, Culture Shock, Chaos UK, Axegrinder, Oi Polloi, Doom, Snuff, Wat Tyler and Doom among the acts to play. Other bands around the same period to gig here include Section 5, Vicious Rumours,

Mega City 4, Senseless Things, Nosferatu and The Dentists. Since the late 1980s gigs here have been few and far between.

After a recent refurbishment the William Morris is currently used by baby groups and dance classes, language schools and for meetings and lectures.

Kensington Town Hall

96 Kensington High St, W8 4SG

Built in 1880 the Town Hall, once known for its classical concerts, hosted a few gigs during the early 1970s.

Acts included Fleetwood Mac, Nazareth, Horslips, Bob Marley and The Wailers, Pink Fairies, Gong, John Martyn, Genesis, Hawkwind, and Chicken Shack. Henry Cow also played a series of concerts under the name Cabaret Voltaire.

The building closed in 1977 when a new town hall had been built to accommodate the merged boroughs of Kensington and Chelsea.

Controversially demolished in 1982 only hours before it was due to be listed the site currently contains a business centre called Kensington Pavilion with a branch of The Ivy restaurant on the ground floor.

Locarno Ballroom

156-160 Streatham Hill, SW2 4RU

The Locarno was one of the first purpose-built ballrooms in the country. It was opened in 1928 by band leader Billy Cotton in front of 1,500 people. Big names of their time such as Glenn Miller, Laurel and Hardy, Charlie Chaplin, Audrey Hepburn and Duke Ellington all appeared here.

Post-war dances were popular with live music provided by Bob Miller, Jeff Rowena and Ted Heath and their respective bands. During the 1960s the Small Faces played here four times and The Move and The Who played three times each. There were also gigs by The Hollies, The Merseys, Chuck Berry, The Troggs, The Easybeats, The Yardbirds and Status Quo.

The building underwent a £100,000 refurbishment in 1970 and reopened as The Cat's Whiskers. The Bay City Rollers and Elvis Costello and The Attractions were among the big names to play over its 14-year life. In 1984 it was re-launched as the Studio Nightclub, then the Ritzy in 1990, and Caesars Nightclub in 1995 with the Three Degrees performing on the opening night. Mica Paris, Dionne Warwick, Crystal Gayle and Barbara Dickson also performed at Caesars though it was more associated with all-inclusive drinks deals, hen parties, boxing events and cage fighting. Brad Pitt was filmed here in Guy Ritchie's film Snatch. An episode of the paranormal television show Most Haunted was filmed here alleging that the building was haunted by ex-hostess Ruth Ellis who worked here during the 1940s. Ellis was later convicted of the murder of her lover and became the last woman to be hanged in the United Kingdom.

Caesars closed in 2010 and was demolished in 2015. Shops and flats have now been built on the site.

Locarno Ballroom

249

Mass/Babalou

St Matthew's Church, Brixton Hill, Brixton, SW2 1JF

St Matthew's is a church that was consecrated in 1824 and during the 1980s it underwent major internal alterations to provide accommodation for a variety of activities, including continued use of a part by the Anglican congregation. The 1,000 people capacity Mass nightclub operated on the 4th floor of the building here from 1996 to 2012 best known for all-nighters at the weekends featuring drum 'n' bass, dubstep and R&B. The venue sometimes put-on live acts

who included 808 State, Tindersticks, Biffy Clyro, Barefoot Contessa, Die So Fluid, Babyshambles, Aeon, Hermann Kopp and Cerebral Bore Metal.

The crypt of the church was run as a separate club called the Bug Bar and later the Babalou which was a restaurant and bar during early evenings while often showcasing smaller bands. The Unknown Quantity, My Heroine, Draygo's Guilt, Purge, In Like Flynn, Paradigm Shift, The Holy Norahs and Bruise all played the Babalou.

Due to debts of the company who leased both Mass and Babalou resulting in forfeiture of the lease, they were repossessed in 2012. The Mass nightclub space is now occupied by the School of Communication Arts and the crypt is now the Gremio de Brixton tapas bar.

New Victoria Theatre

17 Wilton Road, Pimlico, SW1V 1LG

This theatre, adjacent to Victoria Railway Station, opened in 1930 showing both films and variety shows. Some film performances had accompanying performances by big bands. Plans were made for demolition in the 1950s, but it was saved and films continued until 1975.

The theatre also hosted concerts from the 1960s and

acts to have performed here that decade include Buddy Rich and his Orchestra, Tony Bennett, Ella Fitzgerald, The Rolling Stones, The Everly Brothers and Ray Charles and his Orchestra. After closure as a cinema the New Victoria was used more and more as a concert venue with Van Morrison, Diana Ross, Budgie, Freddy Fender, Joan Armatrading, Al Stewart, Slik, Sailor, Heart, Peter Gabriel, Lou Reed, Gary Glitter and Linda Ronstadt all performing here. A live album was released of a 1976 concert here by Daryl Hall and John Oates. At a Judas Priest and Magnum gig in 1977 fans trashed the venue after trouble flared between the audience and bouncers, leading to the venue's closure for a short period. In 1980 Led Zeppelin used the theatre for rehearsals for their European tour.

The venue reopened in 1981 as the Apollo Victoria Theatre with a Shirley Bassey concert. In 1983 there was a benefit concert for Save The Children hosted by Chas and Dave who were joined onstage by Eric Clapton for a few songs. Since then the Apollo has concentrated on large scale long-running West End musicals such as Starlight Express and Wicked.

IMPORTANT ANNOUNCEMENT
DUE TO THE TERRIFIC DEMAND FOR
TICKETS TO HEAR THE WORLD'S GREATEST
BIG BAND, HAROLD DAVISON HAS ARRANGED A
EUROPEAN FAREWELL CONCERT
FOR
COUNT BASIE
AND HIS ORCHESTRA
AT THE
NEW VICTORIA THEATRE
WILTON ROAD, VICTORIA, S.W.1 (Phone : VIC 5732)
FRIDAY, 6th MARCH : 6.40 & 9.0 p.m.
SEATS : 5/-, 7/6, 10/-, 12/6 & 15/-
BOOK NOW

THE NEW VICTORIA THEATRE
The Virgin Concerts presents
DARYL HALL
& JOHN OATES
+ Guests
7.30 p.m. FRIDAY, 3rd OCTOBER
Tickets 75p–£1.75 available from Box Office
and London Theatre Bookings

Odeon Streatham

47-49 Streatham High Road, Streatham, SW16 1PW

This cinema was originally the Astoria Theatre with a seating capacity for over 2,500 people. The grand opening in 1930 showed films plus a variety show with over 100 performers. Internally the film theatre had an Egyptian theme with full stage facilities, a Compton organ with a resident organist, their own orchestra and ten dressing rooms.

In 1955 Peter Sellers came to promote The Ladykillers film. After leaving the stage he re-appeared through a side exit with a tray of ice-creams which he proceeded to throw at the audience. Cliff Richard and The Shadows played a show here in 1959 and in 1961 it was renamed the Odeon after a refurbishment which did away with the Egyptian theme. During the 1960s in addition to the films there were Christmas pantomimes of Cinderella and Aladdin, ballet performances of Swan Lake and The Nutcracker and live bands. In 1963, the Odeon hosted the second night of a 30-date UK package tour featuring The Everly Brothers, Bo Diddley and The Rolling Stones among others. In the book The Rolling Stones I Was There by Richard Houghton a fan recalls Brian Jones throwing an apple core out of the window, and she kept it as a souvenir until it got covered in maggots! Johnny Kidd and The Pirates, The Fourmost and Billy J. Kramer and The Dakotas also played the Odeon in 1963. The 1970s saw live performances by The Four Tops, Stevie Wonder, The Supremes, David Essex, Mud and Ian Dury and the Blockheads who were the last live band to perform there before another refurbishment in 1979, when the cinema was subdivided into multi-screens.

Unlike many other cinema venues in this book that have either succumbed to the wrecking ball or been converted into a gym, church or supermarket, this one is still functioning as a cinema albeit now an eight-screen multiplex and of course, no live music.

DON ARDEN ENTERPRISES LTD. present

THE FABULOUS
EVERLY BROTHERS

BO DIDDLEY
with
'THE DUCHESS' & JEROME

THE
ROLLING STONES

JULIE GRANT

MICKIE MOST ☆ **THE FLINTSTONES**
Compere: **BOB BAIN**

The Pontiac Club

Zeeta House, 200 Upper Richmond Road, Putney, SW15 2SH

Zeeta House opened in 1938 and was originally the main premises of Zeeta and Company who owned a chain of 17 confectionery and catering shops. On the second floor were the Berkeley Rooms, a ballroom with a sprung oak floor where tea dances were held.

After Zeeta was acquired by the House of Fraser who sold off the premises the old ballroom became the Pontiac Club for a couple of years from 1965, open several nights a week geared towards a mod audience with DJs and live acts including residencies from The Action and John Mayall's Bluesbreakers. Other popular acts who appeared at The Pontiac included The Who, The Yardbirds, The Hollies, Them, Jimmy James and The Vagabonds, Carl Douglas Set, Manfred Mann, The Artwoods, The Byrds, Wilson Pickett, The Shevells and T-Bone Walker.

Currently the building is divided between different occupants. The second floor is now offices and many of the original ballroom features have been preserved. The basement which was originally a restaurant is now a nightclub called Le Fez Club.

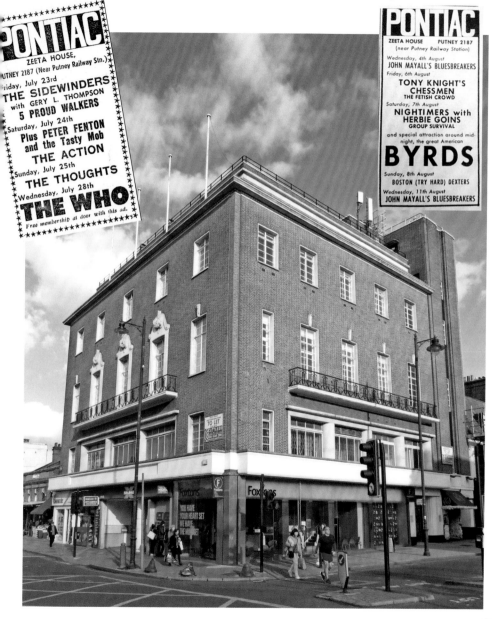

The Pontiac Club

Putney Ballroom

St Mary's Hall, 1 Hotham Road, Putney, SW15 1QS

The Putney Ballroom was the name given to music events from 1959 onwards at St Mary's Hall, a community hall built in 1913. The hall was used for various events including lectures and political meetings such as those addressed by future Prime Ministers Winston Churchill in 1933 and Anthony Eden in 1934.

Some of the first live acts to play here were Vince Taylor and The Playboys, Emile Ford & the Checkmates, Chris Farlowe and The Thunderbirds and The Flee-Rekkers. The Detours played the Putney Ballroom frequently, usually as the support act with seven gigs in 1963, four in 1964 and another two that year after changing their name to The Who. The performance of headline act Johnny Kidd and The Pirates in 1963 left such an impression on Roger Daltrey that it convinced him to switch from lead guitar to vocals. Roger met his first wife that night too. The Detours also supported The Rolling Stones at this venue the same year. Other acts to play here were The Tremeloes, Gene Vincent, Dave Berry and The Cruisers, Johnny Del and The Deltones and Albert Lee before the gigs came to an end in 1965.

Opening from 25th March at
ST. MARY'S HALL,
Hotham Road, Putney, S.W.15

Bingo & Social Club

THURSDAYS, SATURDAYS and SUNDAYS
Doors open 7 o'c. Eyes down 8 o'c.

LARGE CASH PRIZES
FREE GIFTS NIGHTLY

Apply for Membership to:
Hengwyn Bingo Ltd., 45 Castellan Mansions, W.9
Please enrol me for Membership. I am over 18 years of age

Name ....

Address ....

St Mary's Hall was converted into flats during the 1990s and renamed Hotham Hall.

Rainbow Room at Biba

99 Kensington High Street, Kensington, W8 5SA

This was originally Derry and Tom's department store which opened in the 1930s and was famed for having the largest single roof garden in the world which became a huge attraction. The main restaurant, situated on the fifth floor, was called The Rainbow Room. It had an Art Deco oval ceiling lit up with colours of the rainbow, and became popular for dinner dances.

The fashionable Biba store took over the premises in 1973 attracting up to a million customers weekly. The Rainbow Room was sometimes used to put on live acts with New York Dolls, Kilburn and the High Roads, Heavy Metal Kids, Cockney Rebel, Ronnie Spector, Manhattan Transfer and The Pointer

Sisters all performing here. Videos for 'Let's Stick Together' by Bryan Ferry, 'Blue Jean' by David Bowie and 'Devil Gate Drive' by Suzi Quatro were all filmed at the Rainbow Rooms.

The store only had a short life due to financial difficulties, and it closed in 1975. It is now split into various shops and the Rainbow Room is now a gym.

The Roxborough

College Road, Harrow, HA1 1BH

This basement of an old pub close to Harrow on the Hill station was a popular venue for local bands.

The venue's heyday was during the first half of the 1980s when it was the focus for the local punk scene. Some of the bands who played here were 16 Guns, The Meteors, Rubella Ballet, Danse Macabre, Theatre of Hate, Ritual, Butthole Surfers, Subhumans, Blyth Power and UK Subs.

A posthumous release in 2015 called The Roxborough E.P. features recordings by smaller punk bands including The Martyrs and Burning Rhythm plus a live track by Chaos recorded at the Roxborough.

The pub closed in the late 1980s and was demolished along with a row of adjacent Victorian era shops to make way for a new road layout and an office block.

chaos
FIFTH COLUMN

at the
roxbourgh
thurs 19 sept

nearest tube harrow on the hill

THE ROXBROUGH CELLAR BAR
PRESENTS
LIVE ON STAGE
A PARTY NIGHT WITH
MANIC ROCKERS
ORIGINAL SIN. SPARTAN youth

The Roxbrough Cowign Road Harrow Migneser
Nearest Tube Harrow On The Hill (metropolitan line)

Burning
Rhythm
+
Chaos

Live at
the ROXBOROUGH
college rd. Harrow
Harrow-on-the-Hill tube

WED. 8th.
JUNE

onesixsix

Silver Blades Ice Rink

390 Streatham High Road, Streatham, SW16 6HX

Streatham Ice Rink was opened in 1931 with the local newspaper headline proclaiming "Don't go to Switzerland: Come to Streatham". As well as for public skating the rink was used over the years by ice hockey teams and for training by ice skating professionals. In 1962 the rink was taken over by Mecca, who after spend huge amounts on refurbishments, reopened it as Silver Blades.

From 1963 and throughout the rest of the decade, Silver Blades put on live bands of varying degrees of popularity three or four times a week during normal skating sessions. The bands played at the side as people skated around the rink during the performance though occasionally some gigs were so packed that skating was impossible such as when 3,000 people watched The Kinks who played the week their song 'You Really Got Me' was number one in the singles chart. Some of the notable acts that played here include Georgie Fame and The Blue Flames, Alan Price Set, David Bowie and the Lower Third, Small Faces, The Spencer Davis Group, Cream, The Ivy League, Mud, Herman's Hermits, The Troggs, Manfred Mann and The Move. The major stars usually appeared on a Monday, and they used the Bali-Hai nightclub upstairs as dressing rooms. The club was also known for its soul and reggae nights during the 1970s.

The Rink closed in 2011 and was demolished soon afterwards to be replaced by a Tesco supermarket. The new Streatham Ice and Leisure Centre has been built nearby.

The Venue

160-162 Victoria Street, Victoria, SW1E 5LB

This building, situated opposite Victoria Underground Station, first opened as the Metropole Kinema in 1929 and was designed by noted cinema architect George Coles.

The Venue owned by Virgin Records opened in 1978 and advertised itself as "London's Leading Music Club". As well as hosting older established acts plus alternative and new wave chart climbers it was also popular for use by record companies showcasing new signings to the media. The Venue also served food whereby a section of the audience members could be seated at tables eating meals while listening to the acts.

The first act to play The Venue was Graham Parker and The Rumour and every evening for the next few years well-known acts played including Alex Harvey, Blancmange, Depeche Mode, Devo, Hall and Oates, Iggy Pop, Kajagoogoo, Ramones, U2, XTC, The Slits, The Smiths, Chuck Berry, Hanoi Rocks, Tina Turner, Duran Duran and Altered Images. Rory Gallagher was recorded in 1979 for a BBC Radio One In Concert broadcast which was later released as a CD. A show in 1981 by The Skids was broadcast by Capital Radio FM which turned out to be Stuart Adamson's final gig with the band.

The Venue closed in 1984 and the auditorium was demolished. The foyer became occupied by a Dicky Dirt's discount jeans shop and later by on a branch of the Ask Italian restaurant chain prior to its demolition in early 2013 as part of a major redevelopment of the area. The leaded glass ceiling from the foyer was rescued from the demolition and is now installed in the A Slice of Blue restaurant in Clapton, east London.

The building has been replaced with a modern glass office block called Nova South with Greenwood Sports Pub and Kitchen occupying the exact spot of the former Venue.

Wimbledon Palais

10 Abbey Parade, Merton High Street, Merton SW19 1DG

Wimbledon Palais was originally opened in 1909 as a roller-skating rink and then converted for use as a balloon and airship factory during the First World War.

The Palais reopened in 1922 with the largest sprung floor in Europe, hosting live music entertainers, tea-dances, and ballroom dancing competitions. After the Second World War the Palais held popular jazz and dance band events and in 1956 it put on an early rock and roll event with Rory Blackwell and the Rock 'n' Rollers and Leon Bell and the Bell Cats. Many more bands performed here over the next decade at this 3,000 capacity independently owned venue.

House bands were The Chantones and Mike Rabin and The Demons who supported many of the touring acts who appeared here during the 1960s. These included The Rolling Stones, Gene Vincent, The Troggs, The Animals, The Who, Johnny Kidd and the Pirates, The Searchers, The Small Faces, Bo Diddley, The Dave Clark Five, Herman's Hermits, The Kinks and Freddie and the Dreamers. The Beatles played a special afternoon concert here for members of their Southern Area Fan Club in 1963. Not surprisingly the gig was hectic and fans were crushed against a steel cage in front of the stage with policemen trying to push them back as the cage began to buckle under the strain. John Lennon commented "If they press any harder they'll come through as chips." In addition to music events the Palais also hosted wrestling nights.

Radio London and Radio Caroline nights were regularly held here with guest DJs such as Tony Blackburn. The Palais held the Melody Maker National Beat Contest when different groups from all over the country would arrive with coach loads of their fans and perform in front of a panel of judges with heats over an 18-week period. The winners of the talent contest final would receive a Decca recording contract and Vox amplifiers. In 1965, the national press reported that the St. John's Ambulance were overwhelmed dealing with 150 fans that had fainted during a scuffle at the contest's

final at the Palais the night before. A yard at the back of the dance hall was turned into a casualty station. St Louis Union were the winning band that night from judges that included DJ Kenny Everett and a member of The Hollies. Pink Floyd failed to impress during a heat held two months previously.

The Wimbledon Palais closed in 1967 and became a bed and mattress store then offices before being demolished in 2000 and replaced with a parade of shops and flats.

Winning Post

Chertsey Road, Twickenham, Whitton Middlesex, TW2 6LS

The Winning Post is a 1930s pub that was built beside a newly constructed relief road. The pub has a 350 capacity hall that was popular for gigs during the 1970s. Many great acts performed here in the early part of the decade including Status Quo, Mott the Hoople, Hawkwind, Heavy Metal Kids, The Groundhogs and Thin Lizzy who played here seven times. Some of

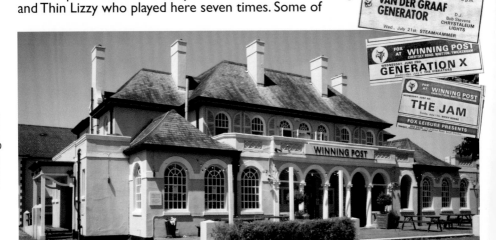

these gigs were promoted by the owners of the Fox record shop in Croydon. By 1977 many punk and new wave acts started to appear here including The Jam, The Saints, The Boomtown Rats, 999, The Vibrators and Buzzcocks. A Generation X gig was reviewed in Sounds who described the venue as a "hostile, plush middle-class pub standing by the side of the two-lane highway rushing its way westwards away from the big city."

The Winning Post is still trading as a pub but since 1977 the number of gigs by original bands has been rare. One standout gig was when remaining members of the Heavy Metal Kids returned in 2011 to play a gig with actor John Altman aka Nick Cotton from Eastenders on guest vocals. Otherwise, the only live music tends to be tribute act such as the Small Fakers, Stated Quo and Planet Abba.

Photos from Paul Talling's
LONDON'S LOST MUSIC VENUES
WALK June 2021

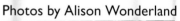

Photos by Alison Wonderland

INDEX

276

...the beginning

SUNDOWN MILE END E3
(Formerly Odeon, Mile End,
Opposite Mile End Underground)
Advance booking Tel: 980-2034

STOP PRESS!
Sold Out

Thursday 7th September
OPENING CONCERT

SLADE

plus

BIGGLES

Wednesday 13th September
ROY WOOD'S WIZZARD
Sam Apple Pie

Thursday 14th September
URIAH HEEP
Sunshine & Mike Marran

Wednesday 20th September
VINEGAR JOE
Stackridge

Thursday 21st September
STATUS QUO/STRAY

Wednesday 27th September
BRINSLEY SCHWARZ/MAN

Thursday 28th September
Performances and Artistes
to be confirmed

SUNDOWN EDMONTON N18
(Formerly Edmonton Regal,
Near Silver St. Main Line Station)
Advance booking Tel: 807-4649

Friday 15th September
OPENING CONCERT

STEPPENWOLF

and introducing

The
John Kay Band

Thursday 21st September

VINEGAR JOE

Stackridge

Friday 22nd September

**Performances and Artistes
to be confirmed**

Thursday 28th September

BRINSLEY
SCHWARZ / MAN

SUNDOWN BRIXTON SW9
(Formerly Astoria, Brixton,
Next to Victoria Line Underground)
Advance booking office Tel: 274-5482

OPENING CONCERT ON SATURDAY SEPTEMBER 30TH
with

DEEP PURPLE

Tickets in advance from Theatre Box Offices.
Open Mon - Sat, 12 noon - 9.00 p.m.

All concert tickets and performance times are also available from all branches of
Edwards & Edwards, Tel: 734 9761 & Virgin Records, Oxford Street, W1, Tel: 580 5755

ACKNOWLEDGEMENTS

In producing this book, I wish to thank Damaged Goods Book's Ian Ballard and Alison Wonderland for design and layout, Duncan Fletcher for proofreading and Simon Strong for the indexing. As with the first volume, without their guidance, hard work and patience this book would not have been possible.

Thank you to the following for their contributions to this book:

Rubberist (Wikimedia): Turnmills photograph (p66)
Ewan Munro (CC BY-SA 2.0): Purple Turtle photograph (p142)
David Jenner: Granada Woolwich interior photograph (p180)
Fernando Pascullo (CC BY-SA 3.0): Earls Court Exhibition Centre photograph (p231)
Gary Bembridge (CC BY 2.0): Earls Court Exhibition Centre photograph (p231)
R Sones (CC BY-SA 2.0): Caesars photograph (p248)
Gary Norgate: Roxborough Harrow photograph (p260).

Thanks also to Symon Jones, Dominic Woodford, Gavin Alexander and Paul Wright for flyers, tickets, etc

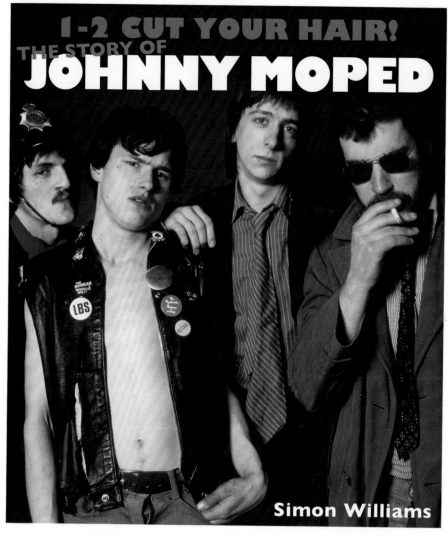

1-2 CUT YOUR HAIR!
THE STORY OF
JOHNNY MOPED

Simon Williams

**The true and crazy story of the legendary first
wave punk band from Croydon, members including
Captain Sensible (The Damned)
and Chrissie Hynde (The Pretenders)**